The Backyard Naturalist

By Craig Tufts

Working for the Nature of Tomorrow®

NATIONAL WILDLIFE FEDERATION
1400 Sixteenth Street, N.W., Washington, D.C. 20036-2266

Table of Contents

The Backyard Naturalist

By Craig Tufts
National Wildlife Federation

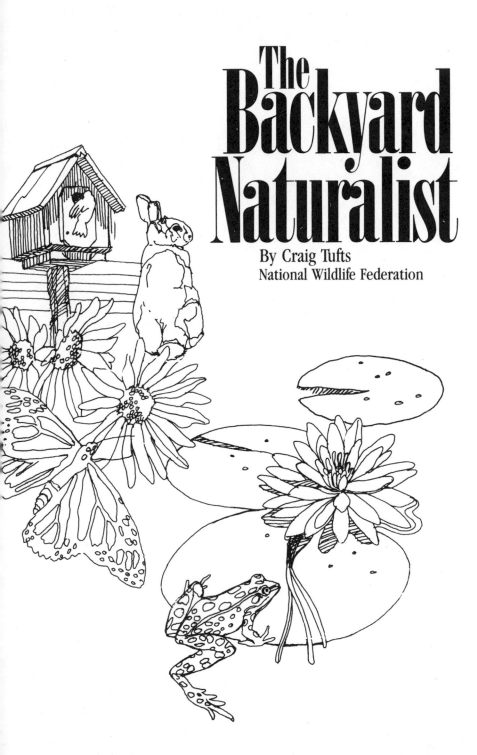

Library of Congress CIP Data

Tufts, Craig.
  The backyard naturalist.

  Includes index.
    1. Wildlife attracting.   2. Birds, Attracting of.
I. Title.
QL59.T84   1988   639.9   88-9966
ISBN 0-912186-93-3

Design by Leslie Eichner LeFranc
Cover Illustration by Frank Fretz
Inside Illustration by George Stump

Chapter One
Making a Place for Wildlife

If you're a gardener, you've experienced that love-hate relationship with your lawn. There's almost nothing that sets off your landscape like a well-maintained lawn. And nothing feels better than stepping out shoeless on a summer morning to wander among the flowers and shrubs.

On the other hand, the time and expense needed to keep your toes happy on that lawn should persuade you to consider reducing the size of your lawn. My own goal is to eliminate much of my lawn, opening up more interesting gardening and recreational opportunities for my family.

There are other important reasons to grow less lawn. Lawn pesticides and fertilizers undoubtedly make their way into ponds and streams. Herbicides and insecticides can kill valuable plants and insects; excess fertilizers foul our waters by causing excess algae.

Most lawn chemicals are dangerous if not applied properly. Even if applied properly, exposure to these chemicals immediately after their application can result in health problems for us, our children, and our pets. So having a smaller lawn and cutting back on the amount of pesticides and fertilizers we use can improve the quality of our air and water.

In my yard, I convert lawn into planting beds very simply. After cutting the lawn in strips of soil with a sharp spade, I turn the sod upside down in place, sprinkle it with granular lime, add two to three inches of soil, an inch of compost and top with three inches of bark mulch. Soon, I have wonderful new soil for shrubs or perennials.

Other options for eliminating lawn include a raised bed vegetable garden, a meadow garden, a mini-orchard, a wildlife-attracting pool, or a new deck from which you can leisurely observe your finished projects.

Your remaining lawn can be a healthier environment if you change the way you maintain it. Surround your lawn with shrub masses and flower beds. Any fertilizer runoff will simply fertilize your other plantings. Keep your lawn small enough and healthy enough so that any weeding can be done with a hand digger, eliminating the use of herbicides.

Always use a grass mixture appropriate to your soil and climate. This will lessen the need for water and fertilizer. In dry western areas, native buffalo grass may be a good choice.

Keep your mower blade sharp and raise or lower it according to the season and growth rate of the grass.

All these changes can mean a healthier environment for your family—and less work for you.

Two years ago, it took me 50 minutes to mow my own yard. This summer, I can mow it in 20 minutes—if I don't stop to pick a strawberry or to visit the butterfly garden. A little less lawn is a healthy, attractive alternative—try it!

Try a Patch of Prairie

Even the most avid gardeners sometimes yearn for a yard that "takes care of itself" and, at the same time, invites wildlife into their lives.

Perfect lawns can, of course, be attractive. But a "flawless" lawn has a price. There's all that watering and mowing! And sometimes we go overboard with chemical pesticides and fertilizers (often applied by a lawn-care firm whose products are not always easy to identify), thereby creating a weedless, insectless (lifeless!) green expanse.

You can bypass the "perfect lawn" hassle without sacrificing the large, sunny, open spaces that lawns afford. *Go natural*. Plant part of your lawn as a meadow or prairie of native grasses and wildflowers.

Once established, your wild yard will be relatively easy to maintain. It will contrast visually with trees and shrubs, and it will attract far more birds, butterflies, and bunnies than ever before.

Your neighbors will probably ooh and aah—especially if you've alerted them early-on to the fascinating plans for your yard. (Alert them, however, *after* you've cleared the way for transforming your property with your local authorities. Make sure no "weed ordinance" or other rules will prohibit you from "going wild.")

How to establish a meadow or prairie. This transformation takes two to three years. The hardest part is preparing a seed bed by killing your lawn with an herbicide in the spring. Next comes rototilling and, perhaps, reapplication of herbicide. Then you can choose one of two ways to establish your meadow or prairie:

• The lengthy (two- to four-year) process. Treat the area as a large planting bed and then gradually introduce (plant-by-plant) native perennial wildflowers and grasses, either grown from cuttings, transplanted from nearby locations (with landowner's permission, of course) or propagated from seed.

• The quicker, easier (but riskier) way. Buy a wildflower or prairie seed mix. It will include both native and non-native plants. The risk: the non-native plants may take over and spread beyond your own property—or they may not prosper at all. However, careful shopping and close attention to instructions on the package can prevent such wayward activity.

Maintenance of a prairie or meadow means you must eliminate weeds that sprouted from seeds exposed during tilling. However, by Year Two, when barren areas are covered by meadow or prairie growth, many weeds, including the noxious ragweed, usually disappear naturally.

With some initial hard work, and mowing once every two years, you'll have a yard that almost maintains itself. And you, your neighbors, and wildlife will enjoy it for years to come.

When I was a kid there seemed to be plenty of neighborhood green spaces to explore: open lots that weren't yet built upon, small streams that wandered through the undeveloped landscape. I remember a tree fort that my brother and I built in the back lot and the observation outpost we fashioned out of cardboard and discarded framing wood that we found down along the river.

For us it was just pure enjoyment. I didn't know I was "having a learning experience," possibly sowing the seeds of my desire to be a naturalist. But lately I've been reading that the best way for kids to learn about the natural environment, to understand a bit about the incredibly complex system in which we're just a few of the cogs, is simply to play in fairly natural surroundings. Such a place need not be a wilderness area. A green, natural place where humans haven't made any effort to sterilize or re-engineer the landscape will do nicely.

Sometimes it looks as if we're moving farther and farther away from giving our children the same chance that we had as kids to meet nature naturally. Our increasingly urban environment seems to gulp up the green spaces.

As an adult, I chose the lot we now live on because of the protected seven acres of common ground that back my property. I knew that over time the natural acres would provide my children with experiences I could never give them within the confines of my small suburban lot. It's a wild area where foxes sometimes venture and where squirrels and moles feel at home. It's a place where cardinals nest and deer occasionally appear.

Some of our newer housing developments, promoting "urban convenience plus rural charm," are sparing a few acres of former farmland or woodland from being built on or paved over. Maybe those of us in older neighborhoods should take a good look at the newer planning and see what we can do to revitalize our bulldozed acreage.

Perhaps you have an opportunity to speak up for the preservation or restoration of natural areas in your neighborhood. Perhaps you can ask where

your homeowners' dues are going, and can point out the problems of trying to maintain "park" spaces. Maybe we should launch a nationwide effort to get a portion of grass areas in parks turned back into fields and scrub and woods, good places for our children and for wildlife.

I can't think of anything that would better encourage our over-urbanized young people to take an early interest in their natural world. Can you? If you agree our natural spaces should be kept intact, then we are indeed on "common ground."

Which Plants for Wildlife?

"Gardening for Wildlife" are words more than 12 million of us toil by. And during this past winter and spring, I, for one, have toiled happily, choosing and now planting roots and seeds that will soon serve my local wildlife surprisingly well.

Some of my choices may likewise suit gardeners who share soils and climate similar to my clayey loam and moderate to cold winters.

I'm gradually using more shrubs and less lawn. Small shrubs and perennials best fill the bill on my 9,000 square feet lot. Butterflies will soon flock to two dwarf buddleias: "Petite Indigo" and "Petite Plum," both introduced by Monrovia Nursery in Azusa, California.

Robins, catbirds, and thrashers will be drawn to the American elderberries, *Sambucus canadensis*, which I propagated last year from hardwood cuttings. I've already heavily pruned the year-old growth and put the cuttings in the landscape. In July, they'll be loaded with small purple-black berries.

A grouping of the native American rose, *Rosa acicularis*, will further improve the good nesting cover for birds in the backyard. This hardy plant, now being tissue-cultured by Knight Hollow Nursery in Michigan, has a dense, upright form, lots of small prickles and thorns, and large, purple flowers. The large rosehips may also prove tasty for some backyard critters.

My perennials serve several purposes: they fill in gaps among my young shrubs, add lots of color, and they attract hummingbirds, butterflies and other insects. This year I've also added hard-leaved and seaside goldenrods, *Solidago rigida* and *S. sempervirens*, terrific late summer butterfly and insect attractors. For the hummingbirds, I've planted two tubular red-flowered perennials: Texas sage, *Salvia coccinea* and a Mexican wildflower, *Galvezia juncea*. But since neither are winter-hardy in my area, I'm growing them as annuals.

The seed catalogs have enticed me to try some new butterfly and hummingbird annuals. "Sunny Red" cosmos, available from a number of suppliers, and "Starfire" marigold from Thompson and Morgan offer the right colors and structure to attract swarms of small butterflies and skippers. I've also planted a new 2.5 foot Mexican sunflower "Goldfinger," orange "Blitz" impatiens, and "Bonfire" scarlet salvia, all available from Park Seed Company.

When you next visit your local garden center, look for cards and plant tags that offer information on attracting wildlife to your property. The National Wildlife Federation and The Planting Council, as part of the "Garden for Wildlife" campaign, have joined forces to bring new and more helpful information on this popular pastime to enthusiastic backyard wildlifers throughout the United States.

Most gardeners have favorite plants; landscape designers do too. With me, favorites include the junipers, a diverse group of ground covers, shrubs, and trees. Some are native to the United States and many have been introduced from Europe and Asia.

For gardeners interested in attracting birds, junipers outshine most other plants in providing cover and food. As evergreens, they're excellent nesting sites and year-round places for birds to hide from predators.

Many produce abundant fruit over a long period of time. Most set their fruit in March and April; some (like the eastern red cedar) mature their fruit the same year. The fruit is ready to eat in August or September and holds for five to eight months, often well into the next fruiting period. That is longer than most other shrubs and trees offer their wildlife-attracting berries.

A native U.S. juniper, the eastern red cedar, *Juniperus virginiana*, provides food regularly for at least 20 or 30 species of birds. A long-lived, sun-loving tree, this "cedar" prefers well-drained soil but can tolerate a wide range of soil pH. It does support a fungus (cedar apple rust) which can damage apples, mountain ash, and other plants in the rose family, but its assets outweigh its drawbacks. Similar juniper species dot the southeastern and south central United States.

Another variety, the Rocky Mountain juniper, *J. scopulorum*, can provide food and cover for many western birds and mammals. The common juniper, *J. communis*, usually a spiny shrub, performs the same life-saving functions in the northern third of the United States.

A juniper of Asian origin popular in the United States and Canada is the

Chinese juniper, *J. chinensis*. It occurs in dozens of forms, from large trees to matlike plants that hug the ground, as well as shrubs such as Pfitzer and Hetzi junipers, widely used as foundation plants. I've seen cedar waxwings dine ravenously on Hetzi berries as late as early May. Many birds use the shrubs for nesting and year-round cover.

Recently I've become interested in a low-growing European juniper sold at many nurseries. It's the Buffalo juniper, *J. sabina*. The plant will, in time, mature at 12 to 18 inches in height, with an 8-foot spread. A female variety, it can probably be pollinated by any male juniper in the area. Many such prostrate junipers bear no fruit, but the Buffalo juniper is a lavish exception. Its

branches make a fine hiding place for small songbirds, shrews, chipmunks, and rabbits.

Many native species of juniper do best in fairly sweet soil, but the Chinese varieties and eastern red cedar tolerate a wide range of soil pH. As a group, almost nothing can beat junipers for providing good habitat for wildlife.

The Attraction of Grasses

Think of "landscaping grasses" and most of us picture an expanse of manicured green lawn. But many other kinds of grasses can be used in place of shrubs or perennials. Tall, graceful, murmuring grasses look great all-year round (with once-a-year cutting), and others can be plucked to make dry-grass arrangements. As a bonus, most grasses are highly attractive to wildlife (especially to birds and butterflies) for both food and shelter.

Meadows and prairies are primarily grasses. The grasses lie thick under the showy meadow wildflowers—sort of like the noodles under a colorful pasta sauce (I am writing this in one of my hungrier moments). At any rate, the flowers give the whole mass flavor and character, while the grasses give a meadow substance and structure.

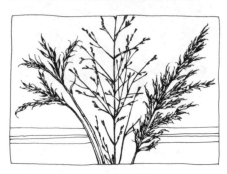

Whether your yard can accommodate a meadow or just a spot or two of decorative grasses, here are some native kinds to consider:

Switch grass (*Panicum virgatum*). A tall (4- to 6-foot), dense-stemmed grass that hisses and rustles pleasingly in winter winds, switch grass is a good soil binder and helps control erosion. Its dense growth makes it good wildlife habitat and its large seeds attract a variety of sparrows. Its bleached blond winter color enhances a landscape.

Big bluestem (*Andropogon gerardi*). Another tall (4- to 6-foot) grass, big bluestem is a mainstay of midwestern United States prairies. As forage, it is as excellent for cattle as it once was for buffalo. Its first leaves in early summer are blue, but its flowering heads are deep purple. Its texture is quite delicate.

Indian grass (*Sorghastrum nutans*). Indian grass is also tall, and is in colorful but subtle bloom in early to mid-August. It sprouts readily in full sun in good warm soil and forms a dense clump, thereby lending itself well to individual plantings. A fascinating feature: when moistened with water, the dried seeds wriggle and writhe, jump and twist—probably a help to these light seeds in reaching the soil through dense prairie thatch.

Broom sedge (*Andropogon virginicus*). A relative of big bluestem, broom sedge is intense pinkish-orange in winter—spectacular against new-fallen snow. Its tiny seeds are relished by a number of sparrow species.

If you'd like to seek out some native grasses available for landscaping you'll find a good resource in *Grasses, an Identification Guide* by Lauren Brown. There's still time this winter to harvest some seeds from nearby meadows or to order seeds from a nursery or mail-order house that sells grasses. Why not give grasses a try?

You say that you want the perfect plant for attracting wildlife to your backyard —just one type to do the whole job?

If that plant did exist, it would be an evergreen, whose branches provide good places year-round to hide. Fruit or seeds would be available all year, relished by desirable birds in your area and despised by wildlife you didn't care for. Its flowers would attract butterflies and hummingbirds. It would have no pest problems.

And it would not be a pest itself, spreading far and wide. It wouldn't cause undue maintenance chores such as cleaning up squishy fruit, raking its leaves or thinning its bushy trunks. And perhaps most important, it would look good all year long.

Such a plant would undoubtedly be without character and boring. Plants that make me work and force me to get to know their qualities are, I think, better for my landscape and wildlife. In caring for them, I make a commitment to constantly monitor and improve my gardening efforts.

Look for plants that offer you and wildlife some of the qualities the perfect plant might provide. Junipers, for instance, meet a good number of the above requirements. Cotoneasters (ka tō' nē as' ters) rank high as varied, desirable, wildlife landscaping shrubs.

Cotoneasters grow well in most U.S. soils. They prosper from the far South to northern areas where winter temperatures do not regularly fall below zero. Some are evergreen, especially in the South. All have numerous white to pinkish-red flowers of small to moderate size. These give way to orange, scarlet, purple, or black fruit in fall and winter. Cotoneasters range in size from mat-forming ground covers to 15 foot high fountain-shaped shrubs.

I grow three species in my yard. You may want to try one or all three.

Bearberry cotoneaster *(Cotoneaster dammeri)*. An evergreen that retains berries into February. A low grower, it spreads by rooting from any branch that has soil contact. "Coral Beauty" is a good cultivar.

Cranberry cotoneaster *(C. apiculatus)*. A shrub with widely arching branches, it tops off at 2 to 3 feet. Although it is deciduous, it has red berries until March.

Spreading cotoneaster *(C. divaricatus)*. A pink-flowered, deciduous shrub growing to 6 feet. It boasts clusters of red fruit for most of the winter.

Although your local garden center may not carry all of the cotoneasters you desire, they will probably carry two or three types. Mail-order houses

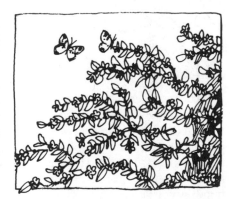

and specialty nurseries carry many others. Do some reading on the varieties that work best in your area and then promise yourself and wildlife that you'll add a cluster or two to your landscape this spring.

Stonewall Mania

Soon after we contracted for our new home to be built, I began the collecting. I had gathered rocks as a boy, cataloging them by type—sedimentary, metamorphic, and my favorite, igneous. Igneous rocks were special because of other childhood interests. Somehow, volcanoes and dinosaurs were wrapped up in those intriguing chunks of pumice and basalt.

My adulthood collection, however, was different. I searched for certain shapes (small slabs, angular blobs) and for colors (reds, grays, near-blacks). I had begun accumulating lumpy detritus that would one day be a backyard rock wall.

Wildlife gardeners might appreciate the nooks and crannies of these man-made mountains more than other gardeners do. From the perspective of a newt or toad, the jumbled bulwark that frames almost a quarter of my lot is home sweet home. Dark, damp crevices provide food, a moist environment, stable temperatures, and secure hiding places from predators.

My rock wall is pretty much home-grown. Three nights a week, we drove to the construction site of our new home, where our basement had been blasted from bedrock. While the kids looked for builder's castaways and my wife inspected the progress to date, I would pick and choose, lift, and lug my newfound gems to a safe corner of the lot. Bit by bit, sandstone slabs and diabase blocks were accumulated. Construction crews viewed me with concern and puzzlement but accepted my harmless, though aberrant, behavior.

Now three years into my construction project, I still add a new rock from time to time—those discovered while putting in the kiwi vines, small boulders unearthed in planting the new river birch, and heirloom rocks from my wife's childhood home.

The rock wall, 3 feet high by 3 to 4 feet wide and 110 feet long, is an integral part of Backyard Wildlife Habitat #2364. My human neighbors have accepted it. The kids billygoat up and down its length. And wildlife has taken notice and moved in.

Shrubs and trees play off its curves, providing food and solace for songbirds and butterflies. Leaves fill up its harsh abutments, softening the angles while nurturing small, crawling creatures. Lichens and mosses are colonizing its sunny surfaces. In years to come, their soft gray and green tones will further soften and enhance the wall.

Rock walls are no spur of the moment project. Materials can be costly if you can't scavenge them. If you are in rocky country and have a strong back, however, they are easily obtained.

Few additions can dress up a home like a well-constructed stone wall. Add some rock to your land. It will beautify your yard and make it a better place for wildlife.

Chapter Two
Feeding Birds

Fall in the air means that soon the birds will be swarming back to our winter feeders. Here are three things we can do to get ready:

Cleaning old feeders. I've been feeding birds all summer, and have just cleaned up the suet feeder, a couple of tubular plastic feeders (which I use for sunflower and niger seed), my hummingbird feeder, and a large feeding table. With the caked-on dirt cleaned off the feeders, the birds can see the seed. Also, a clean feeder reduces the chance that birds could pick up some disease from fungi which collected in the feeder's nooks and crannies during the warm, wet summer months.

How to clean. Usually a mild detergent and a bottle brush are enough for tubular feeders, but caked-on debris may require a good soaking. Rinse well. You might buy plastic feeders that come apart and are easy to clean. I gave my hummingbird feeder a thorough cleaning and put it away for the winter.

An alternative. Buy some new feeders. You may want to try to correct some of the feeder problems you encountered last winter.

Attracting certain birds. If some greedy birds such as grackles and blue jays hogged your feeders last year and drove smaller birds away, try a tubular feeder that lets you vary the length of the perches. Short perches (or none) discourage the bigger birds and are also convenient for the smaller ones. Chickadees, nuthatches, woodpeckers, and a few of the smaller finches need no perch at all.

Thwarting squirrels and other animals. A pole-mounted birdfeeder might thwart squirrels, especially if you put a baffle above and/or below the feeder and place the pole far away from branches that make springboards for the agile squirrels. A costlier feeder, equipped with a spring or a counterbalancing mechanism, will close up under the weight of squirrels and large birds but is not triggered shut when lightweight birds land.

Making feeders. Making feeders is a fun, inexpensive family project. Follow printed plans or design your own.

A feeding table. Provide an open, shallow tray, box, or board that is set 1 to 1 1/2 feet off the ground. All kinds of birds that won't visit any kind of hanging feeder—such as juncos, blue jays, and mourning doves—will feed.

A plastic bleach-bottle feeder. On each side of a bleach bottle, 2 inches from the base, cut two feeding ports (perhaps 3 inches square) for birds to fly into. Put small drainage holes in the bottom and hang from a wire strung through two holes in the bottle's neck. Not as beautiful as a redwood feeder perhaps, but efficient. It will last longer than a plastic milk container which is apt to be affected by sun or cold.

Favorite Feeders and Foods

"Is there one perfect bird feeder?"

"What kind of bird food is best?"

I'm often asked these questions, and I am glad to have the research of Dr. Al Geis, wildlife biologist for the U.S. Fish and Wildlife Service, to back up and expand upon my own observations and experience in feeding birds.

Of course no "perfect" bird feeder or overall best food exists, but we can come pretty close to the ideal.

Bird feeder. Try a tubular, plastic feeder stocked with sunflower seed. You will find fewer squirrels at this feeder than at others, particularly if the feeding "ports" are lined with metal and if you place the feeder away from overhanging eaves and branches. You can choose your perch sizes to suit the kinds of birds you have—or want to have. Long perches can accommodate large birds. Small birds can feed without harassment by larger birds on short perches—or no perches at all.

Bird food. Different birds like different foods, but if there is one favorite, it's bound to be sunflower seed. Sunflower seed (striped or black oil varieties hulled or in the shell) will likely attract purple finches, cardinals, goldfinches, grosbeaks, and other colorful, seed-eating birds. Also, birds such as woodpeckers, titmice, chickadees, and nuthatches, all of which depend heavily on eating insects (adults and larvae) and spiders, will frequent a sunflower seed feeder.

Black oil sunflower seed, with the highest calorie count per gram of kernel, is a fine source of energy, a real necessity for birds when the weather turns cold. The seed is probably a good food substitute for the insect-eaters, especially in certain urban areas where their natural diet may be limited.

Buying seed. You can buy your sunflower seed pre-packaged or loose. Bagged seed (striped or black oil varieties) can be found in most supermarkets, hardware stores, and agricultural co-ops. It's less expensive to buy 25- to 100-pound bags than a smaller size. An even better buy is loose seed that you bag yourself. You get to choose striped or black oil seed, and you get to make sure the seed is clean, not infiltrated with insect-riddled seed, stems, and dirt. *Clean, black oil sunflower seed is your best buy.*

Hulled sunflower seed costs more than unhulled seed, but it's a no-waste food. It both saves your plantings from being smothered in hulls and yourself from having to clean hulls off the ground. As for the birds, hulled sunflower seed means less work to get at the snack that you've put out for them.

For Birds, It's the Berries

Many birds go for berries in a big way. So if you plant a variety of shrubs and trees that bear berries, birds are bound to flock to your backyard.

And think of the bonuses. Berry bushes can double your bird watching fun because the birds that eat berries are apt to be different from the seed-eating birds at your feeder. Plants that bear berries also provide good hiding and nesting places for birds that *don't* eat the berries.

With berry bushes around, watch for hermit and varied thrushes, waxwings, robins, bluebirds, and mockingbirds. Some of your regular seed-eaters such as grosbeaks, cardinals, white-throated sparrows, flickers, purple and house finches, and sapsuckers also eat berries. They may be doubly attracted to your yard by both your feeders and your berry plants.

Here are a few berry-bearing shrubs to consider:

Firethorn *(Pyracantha coccinea)*
Cotoneaster (*Cotoneaster* species)
Staghorn sumac *(Rhus typhina)*
Mountain ash (*Sorbus* species)
Winterberry holly *(Ilex verticillata)*
Eastern redcedar (*Juniperus vir-giniana* varieties)

Most of these plants come in several different sizes, shapes, and horticultural varieties. Look for hardy shrubs that are resistant to locally prominent diseases and that fit well in your overall landscaping scheme. All of the listed plants will bear fruit—though some birds find some varieties tastier than others. Most important, the fruit that ripens in early fall will remain on the shrubs into late winter when wild foods for birds may be scarce.

To find out about an even greater variety of berried shrubs that attract birds, visit your local library. Excellent books on this topic include: *American Wildlife and Plants* by Martin, Zim, and Nelson, *Trees, Vines and Shrubs for Attracting Birds* by DeGraaf and Witman and Ortho's *How to Attract Birds*.

Are you already one of the 60 million Americans busy wooing birds to their backyards (to the tune of about $500 million worth of birdseed, according to a 1980 Fish and Wildlife Service survey)? If not, a good way to start is to join the 12 million people who maintain trees and shrubs (especially berry-bearing plants) for wildlife on their home grounds.

Birdseed—A Mixed Bag

What kind of birdseed mix will best coax birds to your backyard? It all depends on what kinds of birds you like having around. If you don't mind backyard bullies such as grackles, starlings, mourning doves, pigeons, and house sparrows rollicking in your yard, then a common seed mix will do.

But if you want to attract more cardinals, chickadees, goldfinches, juncos, cowbirds, bluejays, red-winged blackbirds, titmice, or white-throated sparrows, you'll choose your birdseed mix more carefully. This is not guesswork but scientific fact, based on research by Dr. Al Geis, an urban biologist for the U.S. Fish and Wildlife Service.

Birdseed mixes most often contain about 10-15 different kinds of seeds. The mixes may all look good and smell good, but you don't want to be led only by your eyes and your nose. What looks like tasty granola to you is not necessarily preferred by the birds you want to attract—and may well bring in the birds many people think of as pests.

Common seed mixes (most prevalent on supermarket shelves and usually least costly) often contain a high proportion of hulled oats, cracked corn, peanut hearts, wheat, and red milo plus some proso millets and sunflower seeds. Cardinals and other birds you particularly want to attract prefer mixes that have lots of proso millets (small white or red beady seeds) and sunflower seeds as well as peanut kernels and fine cracked corn.

Your bird visitors will most appreciate being served their rich mix from a window feeder, from a feeding table placed a foot or two off the ground, or right on the ground. Such a banquet will complement the straight sunflower seed and niger (thistle) seed that you offer the birds from your hanging or pole-mounted feeders—and may double your bird-watching pleasure.

Preferred Seeds of Some Common Birds

American goldfinch—*hulled and oil (black) sunflower; niger*
Blue Jay—*peanut kernels; sunflower*
Cardinal—*sunflower of all types*
Chickadee—*peanut kernels; oil (black) and black-striped sunflower*
Evening grosbeak—*sunflower*
Field sparrow—*white and red proso*
House finch—*oil (black), black-striped, and hulled sunflower; niger*
House (English) sparrow—*white and red proso; German millet*

Mourning dove—*oil (black) sunflower; white and red proso; German millet*
Nuthatches—*black-striped sunflower*
Pine siskin—*sunflower of all types*
Purple finch—*sunflower of all types*
Red-winged blackbird—*white and red proso, German millet*
Song sparrow—*white and red proso*
Tufted titmouse—*black-striped and oil (black) sunflower; peanut kernels*
White-throated sparrow—*sunflower; white and red proso; peanut kernels*

Niger Seed: Black Gold

To many of us, black gold means crude oil. To feeders of birds, however, the price of black niger seed might also bring to mind that same phrase. And like that other black gold, niger seed (or "thistle" as some call it) carries with it a certain amount of intrigue and international mystery.

The seed from *Guizotia abyssinica* comes to us from Ethiopia and Asia, with as much as 70 percent of the 7,500 tons we import annually coming from India. In these nations, many peasants are able to grow niger seed on their small holding of land, and the crop provides an inexpensive cooking oil.

The seed, a distant relative of the sunflower, is fussy about where it grows, preferring long days and warm temperatures. Niger seed matures just a few seeds per plant per day, so harvesting, which must be done by hand, goes on for months.

Growing the crop for birdseed export brings profits to the growers. But because of niger's extended maturation pattern, profits accumulate slowly. That's one reason we pay a high price for these tiny black seeds to which goldfinches and siskins seem addicted.

Many seed crops that come into the United States are required by the Department of Agriculture to be sterilized. This, of course, includes niger seed and there's good reason. As the seeds accumulate in regional holding areas and move toward the ports, they are subject to contamination by unwanted weed seeds. To forestall the possibility of some killer weed sneaking into the United States, the niger seed is sterilized at port-of-entry.

The sterilization itself can create problems that add to seed importers' costs. When seed is steamed in its sacks, mold may develop and spread through the entire batch. That can change the taste and texture of the seed—which may make it unpalatable to birds. So technical problems can affect the cost and availability of niger seed. Political changes can as well.

Those of us who buy niger regularly have watched its price fluctuate with the change in governments in Ethiopia and with the tightening of import restrictions on seed crops.

What's the outlook for the goldfinches' favorite now? I'm glad to report that facilities have been expanded to handle large quantities of niger and to sterilize it by means of a dry process

instead of the steam method. It appears that we'll be able to buy excellent quality, palatable niger seed for the next few years.

As you fill up that tube feeder or thistle sock, you can reflect on where your seed came from and how it was harvested. With a stable market and expanded facilities for dry sterilizing, we should be able to spend less time gasping as we write out checks for bird seed and more time watching birds.

Home-Grown Birdseed

Late summer/early fall is the one time of year we can easily provide home-grown seeds for the birds. No need at this time of the year to rely solely on the vast sunflower, millet, and milo fields of Nebraska or the Dakotas, or the acres of corn in Nebraska, Kansas, or Iowa. Mid-October (and even later) is time enough to start buying birdseed.

Right now, look to your own garden. Resist, if you can, the habit of pinching off fading flowers to keep your plants in full bloom. Instead, let the flowers wither and the seeds swell in their pods. You'll have birdseed to spare, plus enough seed for next year's generation of plants. You'll also have plenty of bloom until frost.

What kinds of plants produce good birdseeds?

Sunflowers, of course, and others in the same daisy family, including Mexican sunflowers *(Tithonia)*. In my yard I let several flowers go to seed near the end of the season. Cosmos and zinnias (the open-pollinated varieties) grow well in the poor soil I am blessed with around my northern Virginia home. They do triple duty: they provide color, they attract butterflies, and when they and some other flowers finally go to seed, they keep my fading garden lively with juncos and finches and several types of sparrows.

Marigolds, too, are multi-purpose. They not only brighten flower beds, they also act as "companion plants" in the vegetable garden (protecting the vegetables from certain pests). And eventually marigolds produce seed the birds love. (All marigolds do this except "mule marigolds," which, like many hybrid plants, rarely produce much good, meaty, fertile seed.)

Four o'clocks (with flowers attractive to hummingbird moths) produce seeds that birds will eat. Cardinals especially seek out the large, black four o'clock seeds that look like tiny hand grenades and probably contain even more kernel than sunflower seeds.

Petunias draw birds to the hundreds of small seeds in their substantial seed pods. In my yard I've watched many a junco hop on a stocky pod, pop it open, and gulp down the tiny seeds.

St. John's worts *(Hypericum)* give a profusion of yellow flowers throughout the summer, and, later, offer a great many seeds.

Prickly pear cacti *(Opuntia)* may attract woodpeckers, and sometimes cardinals and a few other birds that vie for both the juicy pulp and the large seeds inside the cactus fruit.

Letting plants go to seed may give your garden a slightly disreputable look for a short time, but if you can hold off uprooting your annuals until mid-December, you'll give your birds a real treat—and you'll give yourself a brief respite from garden chores and birdseed-buying expenses.

If you'd like to give the local birds a bit of variety in their diet, buy a bag of peanuts. There's no need to provide gourmet food here. The basic roasted-in-the-shell peanut will do for starters. Peanuts are a treat for many wildlife species. Offer them and you'll soon be treated to exceptional performances as the birds and squirrels investigate and partake of this new food.

Squirrels, jays, magpies, and many woodpeckers will make off with all the unshelled peanuts you can offer. Picture a diminutive chipmunk trying to stuff a three-nut unshelled goober into his cheek pouch. Jays hide the peanuts in strange places. Next spring, you can go on a treasure hunt, the course charted by the birds.

Hang a batch of unshelled peanuts in an empty onion bag, suspended well out of the reach of squirrels (if you succeed in doing this, let me know) and you'll create a nifty feeder for small woodpeckers and titmice. How a bird knows that it should land on plastic netting and, with nearly surgical precision, extract a peanut kernel from the shell, I'll never know. I never lose interest in watching the process, however, and perhaps someday I'll come up with an explanation.

For birds with weaker bills, shelled peanuts are a better choice. Buyer beware, however. The bulk seller of bird seed that tries to convince you that the little bitter peanut hearts are the preferred peanut food is either trying to dupe you, or, more likely, just doesn't know what tastes good to most birds.

Dr. Al Geis, who headed the U.S. Fish and Wildlife Service's excellent research program on songbird feeding preferences, found that pieces of peanut kernels were the favorite food of white-throated sparrows, bluejays, and tufted titmice. The hearts, however, the peanut product most commonly found for sale in bird feeding specialty stores, were highly attractive only to starlings, a species most people do not welcome at their feeder.

Chopped peanut kernels are terrific sources of protein and fats for some birds that infrequently visit feeders. Thrashers, thrushes, creepers, wrens, some warblers, and some of the smaller sparrows will search diligently for small bits of peanut at your feeders or on the ground.

I continually ask my bird seed supplier for peanut kernels but to no avail. I've thought of labelling their peanut hearts barrel with a glossy photo of a

starling with the caption, "Feed me my favorite" but have decided on the soft sell instead. I'll bet that there is a "not for human consumption grade" peanut out there just waiting to feed a hungry titmouse. In the meantime, try adding peanuts to your feeding menu. Wildlife will appreciate the occasional special snack and I can guarantee that you'll be entertained by their visits.

In Winter, Do It With Suet

One of the best cold-weather bird foods is suet, a dense beef fat. A winter suet feeder in your yard invites birds to which you otherwise might never play host. Suet, a valuable addition to your bird feeding program, provides birds with the extra energy they need to stay warm in winter.

From late fall through early spring, I buy three pounds of suet at a time and freeze it in half-pound chunks. That way, my suet feeder never runs low. You can usually find suet at a supermarket or (if you want to be sure you're getting *real* beef suet) at your local butcher shop.

Most suet feeders are wire mesh cages. The mesh needs to be just large enough for a hungry bird's bill to reach through, but not so large that a crow or raccoon could make off with large pieces of suet.

A suet cage should be constructed of plastic-coated wire instead of uncoated metal. The plastic eliminates the possibility that any part of a bird would freeze to the uncoated surface. The cage needs a back door for inserting the suet. You can find suet cages for sale, or you can make your own.

Hang your feeder from the trunk or branch of a tree. A suet cage 6 or 8 feet off the ground will regularly attract woodpeckers, chickadees, nuthatches,

titmice, perhaps brown creepers, and other birds that find suet a good substitute for their natural high-energy foods (insect eggs, larvae, etc.). At this height, the feeder is out of reach of skunks, foxes, and dogs, though I won't guarantee that a raccoon or an opossum won't raid the cage.

European starlings are suet-loving birds who are all too apt to take over your whole yard. If you live in starling country, you can try to starling-proof a suet cage, thereby discouraging an unwanted invasion.

Suspend a baffle (a pie tin may do) or plastic dome over the feeder. Unlike nuthatches, chickadees and such, starlings are not very good at hanging vertically or upside-down to feed; they prefer to perch on the top.

Another trick is to buy or make a double-mesh cage. The wire basket that holds suet fits inside a cage of larger mesh (1 to 1 1/2-inch). The small birds can hop in and reach the inner basket but larger birds (including starlings) cannot.

On the coldest of days, your suet feeder may draw birds that rarely visit any kind of feeder. During such frigid weather, we receive reports of Carolina wrens, red-shouldered hawks, pileated woodpeckers, juncos, thrashers, American kestrels, and yellow-rumped warblers visiting backyard suet feeders.

So don't let cold weather get you down or hamper your winter bird-feeding efforts. Put out the suet and watch the delightful scene as birds vigorously energize themselves.

Christmas for the Birds

Thinking "Christmas tree" in February may seem unseasonable, but an evergreen planted in that month (or as early as the ground thaws) will be thriving next December, and it probably will be decorated with birds. You won't have to add an ornament or a light.

Planting evergreens is one of the best things you can do for your landscape—and for wildlife. Strategically placed, an evergreen does triple duty: it shields your home from harsh winds; it beautifies your yard; and its dense foliage also provides protection for wildlife—especially for songbirds. By putting evergreens in your yard, you extend a direct invitation to the birds.

Songbirds revel in brushy evergreen growth. They use it as a buffer against the wind and as shelter from the snow. You yourself can test the protection the foliage offers against the wind. Some blustery day, find a pine, spruce, fir, hemlock, holly, or cedar tree. Stand on the cold, windward side a few minutes; then go around to the downwind side. There's quite a difference. You'll find the protected side remarkably comfortable—and so do the birds.

In evergreen boughs the birds also find protection from hawks, cats, and other predators. And some evergreens provide food for the birds. Try the Rocky Mountain juniper (*J. scopulorum*), the Eastern redcedar (*Juniperus virginiana*), the Nellie Stevens, American, and Fosteri hollies (*Ilex* species and hybrids), and hemlocks (*Tsuga* species).

Some deciduous trees do well when planted in the fall, but spring is the best time of year to plant evergreens. They need the summer and fall months to establish their roots before winter.

In planning your evergreen plantings, here are a few things to consider:
• Choose a tree well suited to your climate. Consult your local garden center to determine what plants are hardy in your area.
• Choose a tree that can be sheared. Shearing helps create even greater foliage density than would naturally occur. It also allows you to shape the tree to your liking.
• Allow space for the tree to grow freely. Remember that even a sheared tree may grow to be as much as 15 feet in diameter.

• If feasible, plant your tree north or northwest of your house. That location will block winter winds and possibly lower your heating costs.
• For optimum enjoyment, plant the tree where your view of it from the house is unobstructed. Then keep your binoculars by the window to feast your eyes on the birds that are sure to be visiting your "Christmas tree" all year round.

A Holiday Treat

This season I plan on making a holiday tree for the birds. I'm bypassing the evergreen that is decorated with the usual strings of popcorn or cranberries. Those traditional "bird trees" do look festive, but, to tell you the truth, I've never noticed birds eating the decorations. Have you? So this year, I'm going to experiment with a real banquet for the birds. Rather than festooning an evergreen, I am going to adorn the bare branches of a deciduous tree. You could decorate either a tree growing in your yard or a cut one placed where birds are most apt to notice it.

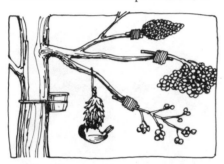

Choose a sturdy, 5- to 10-foot tree with sparsely-spaced branches. Then collect several kinds of berry-bearing clippings. Using small-guage copper wire, attach the clippings toward the ends of the tree branches, making it look as if the clippings belong there.

Berry-bearing plants vary from area to area. The color red is, of course, a must in any holiday decorating, and here in Virginia, I'm using mountain ashes and staghorn sumac. Then I'm adding some deciduous hollies (especially possum haw or winterberry), and some multiflora rose sprigs. (I dip the freshly cut tip of all sprigs in melted paraffin to keep the fruit from drying out too fast.) Magnolia berries are among the best foods for robins and other thrushes.

Orange-toned bittersweet and pyracantha also make bright splashes of color, balanced by gray juniper berries and the black or blue berries of large viburnums. Snowberry fruit provides a contrasting white accent. I'm including a few wild grapes, not for their looks (dry and shriveled) but because I know that robins, bluebirds, and mockingbirds enjoy this winter fare.

My tree includes several pine and spruce cones filled with a suet-peanut butter mixture for nuthatches, chickadees, and maybe a titmouse or two.

If you can't obtain pine cones, perhaps you'll be able to use the conelike structures from large magnolia trees. Once the red berries are gone, the big cones (plus 4 or 5 inches of stem) can be dipped in a suet-peanut butter mixture and hung by wire, like single tree ornaments. The small, conelike fruits of the sweetgum tree *Liquidambar* can be plucked of their gumball "points" to make cratered structures which can be packed with a suet mixture and wired to the tree.

A holiday tree isn't complete without a string of something intertwined through some branches. I'm hanging short strings of pitted dates, high-sugar food for bluebirds and mockingbirds. I'm also wiring small containers of raisins to the tree trunk.

With our bird tree complete, my family can really celebrate the holidays, watching from the window to see which birds eat what.

Early fall is the best time to reevaluate the placement of your bird feeders. A feeder's location should be convenient and highly visible for you and safe and secure for the birds.

All of us enjoy the antics of small seed-eating winter visitors. Nuthatches, chickadees, goldfinches, and the "red" finches will eagerly come to round plastic feeders or pole-mounted tubular feeders filled with sunflower seed. Place these feeders at least four feet from the ground. Nearby dense shrubs or small trees offer perches for birds visiting the feeder. Chickadees and nuthatches need tree limbs against which they can hull sunflower seed.

More birds seek out suet in winter than any other single type of food. Place it in plastic-coated wire mesh holders. Hang these from tree limbs or mount them on a *dead* tree trunk. Suet feeders placed on healthy trees invite the rapid invasion of tree-damaging insects and fungi. Don't place suet too close to a window unless you enjoy washing windows. Birds flick pieces of suet off their bills, making a greasy mess of the glass.

The best type of feeder for attracting ground feeders, birds that feed in groups, or squirrels is a simple feeding table. Place this feeder on a pole that raises it 12 to 18 inches above the ground. Cat-concealing cover should be at least 10 feet away. Good quality mixed birdseed consisting of proso millets, sunflower, and perhaps a bit of cracked corn, hulled sunflower, and peanut pieces will keep the greatest number and variety of birds at this feeder. I use a 2- by 3-foot piece of marine plywood edged with molding and mounted on a post 4 inches in diameter as a serviceable feeding table.

I've given you ideas about feeder types, locations, and foods to put in them. Let's look at one safety consideration, from a bird's point of view. Although we want to view birds clearly and comfortably from inside our warm homes, feeders are best located either very close to our windows or a good distance—at least 30 feet—from them. Such placement may prevent birds from colliding with your windows. Place feeders far enough from windows so that birds have space to fly away if they get frightened.

You might take a bird's eye view of your windows from your feeder's location during key feeding times—early morning and late afternoon. Look toward your house. If what you see appears to be something you would want to fly into if you were a bird, move the feeder to a less appealing location.

You will find homebound birdwatching more enjoyable this winter by fine tuning your feeding program right now. I hope your winter birding season is a great one.

Summer Bird Feeding

Why, you may ask, should anyone feed birds in the summer? Don't they get enough seed, fruit, and insects on their own? Probably, yes—if you're talking "survival." But there's no reason *not* to offer the seed, fruit, and other food that will draw birds to your yard all year.

Summer visitors are apt to be a different mix from birds that you enjoy in winter. Some of the winter ones will stay, but some summer birds aren't around in the winter and might not come to your yard in the summer except for the food you provide. Many young birds, too, come to feed with their parents in summer, and watching bird families is a rare treat: parents teaching their young to eat, family squabbles, perhaps a "runt" learning to get its fair share of food.

With some exceptions, the same kinds of food you put out in winter will serve the birds well in summer.

Seed. Sunflower seeds are a mainstay, but try standard mixtures with a high percentage of proso millets, sunflower seed, and some cracked corn. They will draw many seed-eaters and their young. Chickadees and titmice are especially entertaining to watch as their families of four to seven fledglings learn the ropes.

Fruits. Citrus fruits, plus bananas, pieces of apple, and raisins, are not *necessary* food. But in many parts of the country, a fruit salad will likely bring in orioles, house finches, grosbeaks, and tanagers. Fruits are almost sure to draw mockingbirds, thrashers, and catbirds (which rarely visit northern feeders in winter). Even woodpeckers, which normally subsist on a diet of insects, may avidly take fruit. Many seed-eaters, in fact, eat fruit and other foods as well.

Sugar water. A four-to-one mixture of water and sugar, placed in small, plastic vials, wired to shrubs and trees, will likely draw not only hummingbirds but a number of other birds. A purplish solution of water and grape jelly may attract treetop-inhabiting orioles (the Baltimore in the East; Bullock's and other species in the West), especially if you have large trees in or adjacent to your yard.

Exceptions to winter foods in summer. Unless you live in the far north, there's no need to offer suet and rendered-fat foods such as seed balls or peanut butter mixtures. They'll probably melt. Besides, a summer insect diet gives the birds the high-fat content that suet provides in the wintertime.

So, with one eye on your food budget and the other on your bird feeders, enjoy the backyard picnic all summer long.

Chapter Three

Who's Who Among Your Backyard Birds

Seeing Red—And Liking It

That redbird with the big beak really has it made. During the holidays, just about everyone receives its picture—it might be the number one Christmas card pinup. The northern cardinal, as this bird is officially called, is popular for good reason.

No other bird I know of looks so good against freshly fallen snow. Both the male and the female sing a pleasant, simple song, often countersung (the male answers the female on a slightly different pitch). And cardinals seem to prosper with the alteration of habitat that accompanies our home building efforts. Few other songbirds reward us so richly or so rapidly if we but scatter a few handfuls of sunflower seed onto the ground or on a low feeding table.

The cardinal ranges throughout most of the eastern and central states, the entire South, and much of the arid Southwest. It is so popular that even those who live where the cardinal does not—California, the Rocky Mountain states, and the Pacific Northwest—love the bird and very much want it to visit their yard. The cardinal may be the ideal suburban bird.

Cardinals prefer dense, shrubby habitat. Provide that in your Backyard Wildlife Habitat and you can keep a pair happy. They nest in shrubs and viney tangles at least twice every summer. If the shrubs (such as junipers, dogwoods, honeysuckles, and viburnums) provide fruit—all the better.

In the winter, this bird with a very heavy, crushing bill prefers sunflower seed. Offer it on a feeder close to the ground; cardinals do not like to feed high or far from dense cover. They are invariably the last birds to leave the feeder each evening.

These birds do have some qualities that might be considered negative. They can become bullies at feeders, forcing smaller sunflower aficionados away for a brief time.

And their territoriality can prove annoying. Anyone who has put up with a pair of cardinals constantly battering themselves against a house window throughout the entire nesting season soon questions the birds' common sense. The bird is simply trying to keep invaders out of its territory, but doesn't realize it is seeing a reflected image in the window. Block the reflected image, and the cardinals should turn more peaceful.

Cardinals have greatly increased their breeding range over the past 80 years and now appear with regularity throughout much of New England and southern Canada. Cardinals do not migrate, but simply keep pushing farther north and west as new suburbs and bird feeders proliferate. Cardinal lovers now on the edge of the bird's range need only wait, plant some dense shrubs, and entice new colonists with sunflower seeds.

Chickadees, Chickadees

Almost all of us know a black-capped chickadee when we see one. The little bird with the black cap and black bib is a regular to many American backyards.

Lesser-known chickadees abound as well—six other species in the continental United States. In my own neck of the woods in eastern Virginia, we see the Carolina chickadee. Its range is almost as great as that of the black-capped chickadee. Other species are less widespread and less recognizable, at least until their identifying marks become familiar.

The mountain chickadee, with a black mask over its eyes and a thin white stripe above, ranges over the western mountain region.

The chestnut-backed chickadee, the most colorful United States chickadee, lives in the Pacific northwest. The Siberian tit lives in extreme northwest Canada, Siberia, and on the tundra edge in north central Alaska. The boreal chickadee lives throughout much of Canada and Alaska, and occasionally nests in the northernmost tier of the lower 48 states. It sometimes visits feeders further south. The Mexican chickadee's range in the United States is limited to two mountain ranges on the Arizona/New Mexico border.

Common or uncommon species, chickadees are a joy to have around. You can best entice them to your yard if you have trees, can provide a feeder full of sunflower seed (chickadees also eat suet), and put up nest boxes.

The chickadees that feed on sunflower seed and suet all winter will raise families in the spring (usually five to seven eggs per family). The parents will bring their young back to the feeders in the summer.

By the following winter the young will have fit into their non-nesting-time social structure. These social groups usually consist of 5 to 14 chickadees traveling through woodlands in the company of such other species as nuthatches, woodpeckers, and kinglets.

At nesting time, March through June, chickadees take up residence in natural tree cavities or often in bluebird nest boxes. You may, however, wish to build a special chickadee house with a 1 to 1 1/4-inch entrance hole, smaller than that required by a bluebird. You'll want to place the box on a metal pole or a tree, on the edge of a woodland or within the woods.

You'll notice that chickadees build nests with moss, even when they have to haul it a distance. That raises a few questions: Why moss? Does it have some insecticidal value? (Scientists are finding that some bird species build nests with plant leaves that ward off parasites.) And: Do chickadees in Virginia and Arizona use the same kind of moss in their nests? Intriguing!

You can aim toward putting together a box for chickadees that will be ready for fall—the perfect time to put a nest box in its proper place.

If you've heard the phrase "sitting in the catbird seat," you may have wondered, as I have, how the catbird fits into this picture of someone sitting in a position of power.

For those of us who know catbirds as wary inhabitants of low-lying scrub, the phrase makes little sense. About the only time catbirds act "powerful" is when they're proclaiming their territory. Most of the time they're barely noticeable.

You'll hear their mewing, catlike call that gives them their name. Or you'll hear a rapid, jumbled song like a mockingbird's (catbirds are related to thrashers and mockingbirds).

They seem to be one of the gentlest of our songbirds, and I've never really understood why some people dislike catbirds. I've heard it said that they pick on the young of other birds, but they're not known as nest robbers. They're certainly not going to stalk and pounce, catlike, on us—though I've been harassed more than once by a protective parent when I approached a nest.

My most vivid childhood memory of catbirds is having them eat raisins from my outstretched hand. Catbirds love fruit, more than almost any other bird I've come in contact with. I've banded numerous catbirds in late summer and early fall. Most of them are loaded up with the fruit of elderberries, pokeweed, black tupelo, or some other juicy fruit.

You can easily entice summer catbirds to your yard using a tray stocked with raisins. They'll also feast on your blackberries, raspberries, blueberries, and grapes. You'll want to protect *your* family's supply of berries with well-anchored bird-proof netting. In my own yard, I'm creating fruit-bearing hedgerows that flank adjoining properties. In time, these hedgerows will be home for a pair of catbirds and their family.

Increasingly, it appears that more catbirds are wintering farther north. However, to survive the harsh temperatures and snows, they need the fruit of fall and winter-bearing trees, shrubs, and vines. Provide part of such a fruit diet with shrubs and trees in your yard and augment it with finely-chopped fruit and shredded suet. Place these supplemental foods in dense habitat

such as the viney tangles the birds tend to prefer in the winter.

I've begun to wonder if catbirds are extremely fragile birds. Though I mark hundreds of them each year, few seem to return to the place where they were originally banded. Are they less capable than other birds of returning to a specific home territory? I wonder if perhaps they'd be better off if, instead of flying from place to place, they did *indeed* sit in the catbird seat.

Jenny Wren

Jenny Wren and her boyfriend are stick stuffers. But don't let that keep you from trying to persuade these bug-eating bundles of brown fluff to nest in your backyard.

The house wren, also known as "Jenny," is a diminutive, mousy songster that can be found throughout much of the United States. Look for it darting in and out of viney tangles and brush piles, voicing a buzzy chatter.

Perhaps no other bird in our urban areas lends such a cheerful, bubbling note to early spring mornings. It may only be a winter visitor to people living in the Deep South, however.

House wrens eat insects. Much of their diet consists of very small creatures that hide by day in brush, tangles, and dead wood. Bugs, the insect family that includes a number of garden pests, are the wren's favorite snack. Its diet, however, is diverse, and may include troublesome insects such as caterpillars, beetles, and grasshoppers.

If you wish to have a native bird nest in your yard, build a wren box. As with any other type of nest box you place in your backyard wildlife habitat, build it properly. Wrens are not fussy; a box 4 by 4 inches and 6 inches high inside is perfect. Place the 1-inch entry hole an inch below the top. Be sure to build your birdhouse so that the top or side can easily be removed for cleaning. A nest box that is not carefully watched and cleaned is probably worse than no nest box at all.

If you build nest boxes for your yard, you also need to know something of the house wren's habits. Father wren arrives back at his breeding territory in spring and immediately begins to sing and scout. His bubbling song rings from every brush pile and fence post. And his inquisitive nature leads him to every nest box in your yard.

In preparation for his mate's arrival and her critical appraisal, the male wren constructs "dummy" nests in three to five suitable places. One male wren can stuff every nest box you have with sticks in two days. The female wren will choose one of the nests and will finalize the nursery with a lining of more delicate or perhaps more comfortable materials.

As a nest-box watcher, your duties include cleaning out the unused nests as soon as the wrens have selected their nesting site. House wrens will often nest twice each summer, so keep up your cleaning duty for the duration.

You can enjoy a great review of this feathered dynamo's courtship behavior in Donald Stokes' *A Guide to Bird Behavior I.*

House wrens are truly helpers in the garden, and I, for one, can use all the help I can find. Put a wren house up in your yard, then sit back and enjoy the antics of your new neighbor.

Mockingbirds are amazing. Virtually no other familiar bird sings such an incredibly varied song so noisily at such frequent intervals. And surely no other common bird defends its territory more aggressively.

Mockingbirds can inspire admiration, anger—and occasionally downright belligerence. Their antics have long been known in the South. Yet over the past 30 years, northerners, too, have become acquainted with "mockers" as the birds have pushed north (as far as Maine and southern Canada). Apparently they have been attracted by an increasing abundance of suburban berry-bearing shrubbery. They've become a delight and/or an aggravation to a whole new audience.

Mockingbirds definitely do things their own way. Most birds confine their territory-marking to breeding seasons, usually when the male delineates "his" chunk of earth by moving from perch to perch and vocalizing.

Not so among mockingbirds. The female as well as the male will defend its winter territory against raids on its stashes of food such as berries and other fruits. If your bird feeder happens to lie within a mockingbird's territory, you can expect to see the mockingbird chase other birds, even physically attack them, even though a mockingbird itself generally will not use a seed feeder.

Such behavior can be especially distressing if you're trying to attract, feed, and house bluebirds. But there's a remedy. In late fall, both bluebirds and mockingbirds shift their diets from insects to fruit. Encourage bluebirds to remain in your yard through the winter by stocking an empty nest box with raisins. The bluebirds will investigate the box and discover the food. The mockingbirds will likely never catch on that a favorite food is inside.

On the mockingbirds' plus side is the entertaining performance they can put on in search of food, in defense of their territory, or during courtship. You can't dispute the charm of their song, no matter how loud and long.

And you can't help being amused when you see a mockingbird "wing-flashing." It goes into its act on the ground, stretching its wings forward in a stuttering manner. It's thought that on a sunny day, the shadow of the fluttering wings may spook insects out of

the grass. When the bird spots a bug, it races roadrunner-fashion or flutters into the air to grab a flushed insect.

To attract mockingbirds all winter, plant fruit-bearing trees and shrubs such as dogwoods, viburnums, hollies, mistletoe, or junipers. Multiflora rose is, in many areas, the mainstay of the mockingbird's winter diet. But multiflora rose matches the mockingbird in aggressiveness and, in most areas, has been labeled a pest. Like the mockingbird, it has its downside, but both the mocker and the multiflora may deserve a place in your backyard.

Hummingbirds See Red

Hummingbirds in your garden create a breathless sort of beauty. In the blur of their humming, fast-beating wings, the small (smallest in the world) birds hover over flowers, lapping up nectar with their brush-coated tongues. These aerial acrobats dart from flower to flower, sometimes even flying backward. They shimmer with iridescent colors that come not from pigment in the birds' feathers, but from light striking the feathers' prism-like surfaces.

Do you want "hummers" in your backyard? Let your garden break out in a riot of color. Hummingbirds are suckers (so to speak) for tubular red, orange, and pink flowers. Any yard flaunting a perpetual gaudy bloom will probably attract many hummingbirds on their migrations in both spring (late March to mid-May, depending on your distance from their wintering habitats in Mexico and the Caribbean) and fall. And if you have the right habitat for nesting, you may have hummingbirds with you the whole season.

While you can coax hummingbirds to your yard with sugarwater feeders or dense foliage for nesting, flowers are probably your best lures. Although hummingbirds in North America also feed on small insects (ants, thrips, and insect larvae) found on or near flowers, flower nectar makes up their main diet. Many kinds of annual and perennial flowers, available as seeds and young plants, attract hummingbirds. Purchase them at garden centers or through a mail-order nursery. Some suggestions: scarlet salvia (perhaps overall the most available and effective hummingbird plant); scarlet or pink petunia; scarlet morning-glory; and scarlet nicotiana (also called flowering tobacco), which also attracts day-flying bumble bee moths and hummingbird moths, and night-flying hawk moths.

Hummingbirds are especially fond of wildflowers. Buy them from reputable nurseries or from your local or state plant societies. Such suppliers are careful to make native perennial wildflowers available without depleting our natural wildflower supplies. In the East, cardinal flower (*Lobelia cardinalis*) and trumpet creeper (*Campsis radicans*) or its hybrids are good choices. In the western states, scarlet paintbrushes (*Castillija*), Pacific Northwest columbine (*Aquilegia formosa*), red flowering currant, or scarlet pensemons are highly attractive.

In the eastern United States, look for the ruby-throated hummingbird, the only hummer commonly found east of the Mississippi. In the Rockies, look for black-chinned, broad-tailed, and calliope hummingbirds. The rufous, Allen's, and Anna's hummers are predominantly Pacific slope breeders. The hummingbird capital of the United States is southeastern Arizona, where 15 kinds of hummingbirds might be seen beating their way from flower to bright flower, all day long.

Suppose you want hummingbirds to visit your backyard but, for one reason or another, you cannot provide the bright-colored flowers that best attract them. Must you go hummingbirdless the rest of your life? Not necessarily. In fact, many people try to attract "hummers" solely by placing feeders around the yard.

Nutritionally, feeders are not ideal for hummingbirds. If properly stocked and maintained, however, they can provide good food supplements and the birds will visit them. If you opt for feeders, here are some tips:

Feeders. Choose a bright red plastic feeder, since hummingbirds are strongly attracted to the color red. Failing that, dress the feeder in a red bow or sock; or place a red bow nearby. Anything red will catch a hummingbird's eye. Make sure the feeder comes apart easily so that regular cleaning will be simple.

Placement of feeders. Hang a feeder where you can see it easily from your window or deck, but not so close to a window that the hummingbirds will fly at their own images reflected in the glass. That is a major cause of hummingbirds' deaths around homes, and one that is easily preventable.

Food. Mix four parts of water to one part table sugar, heated only long enough to dissolve the sugar. A higher sugar concentration than four parts water to one part sugar can, in the long run, cause kidney or liver damage in hummingbirds. Some people add red food coloring to the water, but you don't need to. Just be sure your feeder itself is, in part, red. Store the leftover sugar-water in the refrigerator in a clean glass or plastic container.

Feeder care. Feeders need cleaning every three days to prevent the sugar-water solution from fermenting, which might harm the visiting hummingbirds. When you are on vacation and can't keep the feeder clean, it's better to take it down.

Nesting habitats. Hummingbirds nest in a variety of habitats throughout the United States, many in the mountainous West or in deserts; others in deciduous or evergreen forests across southern Canada and throughout the

United States. To be a hummingbird host you might also consider their nesting needs.

A nesting box will not lure hummingbirds, but several evergreen or deciduous trees and shrubs may encourage the birds to nest in your yard. They'll build in dense foliage, usually in the fork of a very small limb. They make their tiny, camouflaged nests of spider webs, hair, bits of lichen and other materials. If you're lucky enough to get nesters, you can be sure to hold their attention with flowers and birdfeeders—and perhaps a sprinkler or shallow pool for baths.

Which Birds Are Back?

"Are the blue jays in the yard this winter the same blue jays that brought their young to our feeders last summer?"

"Is the junco at the feeder the one that came last year? It has the same odd, white feathers on one wing!"

Hardly a month goes by without a letter asking me: *How* can you tell if this year's birds are the same friends from other seasons? It's not easy. Few birds have identifying differences in plumage. Behavior, however, might give you a clue. I heard about a catbird that showed up every spring at the same window for a ration of raisins. That one is apt to be the same bird, back at a familiar station.

Banding birds is the only *sure* way I know to tell one individual from another. That doesn't mean that just anybody can rush out and capture a bird to put a band on its leg. Birdbanders have to be trained and must be licensed by the United States Fish and Wildlife Service. I underwent a fairly rigorous apprenticeship with an expert bander. It's a delicate business to catch a bird, without harming it or seriously frightening it, and to slip a small, numbered aluminum band on its leg.

Often birds are trapped in a special "mist net"—again, only with the permission of the United States Fish and Wildlife Service. Such nets are hung along travel routes in birds' habitats. Nets differ in size (usually 6 to 8 feet high and 40 feet wide) and color, depending on the habitat and the topography of the banding site.

Banding has answered for me the question about returnees: Yes, some birds do come back—for two, three, four, even ten years. Our own resident bluebirds, cardinals, chickadees, and titmice are apparently going to be in our area throughout their lives. One cardinal we banded in 1975 was caught again six years later—20 feet from where it was first caught.

Birdbanding is more than a hobby, of course. It's a scientific endeavor that helps us learn how birds age, where they go, and what their social structure is. Tracking and counting birds have pinpointed two problems that contribute to our diminishing bird populations: rapid destruction of rain forests in Central and South America (wintering habitats for many species of songbirds); and problems (perhaps caused by acid rain and other airborne toxics) on the northern breeding grounds of many of the same songbirds.

My own birdbanding has indicated the great need to maintain scrub habitats in our suburbs. They provide winter cover and food for birds like juncos and white-throated sparrows and summer cover, fruit, and insects for breeding birds such as prairie warblers.

My next banding experiment: to see if the summer goldfinches and song sparrows are the same ones that visit my feeders in winter.

Chapter Four
Making Other Visitors Welcome

To most people, "Gardening With Wildlife" is apt to mean inviting birds to a banquet, or perhaps being visited by inveterate gate-crashers such as rabbits and squirrels. But there are highly desirable guests that respond beautifully to proper invitations: *butterflies*.

Flowers and birds bring color and life to a garden, but lively, colorful butterflies add a delicate grace note as nothing else can.

What kinds of invitations entice butterflies? A few particular plants, well positioned in your yard. Butterflies are drawn to:
• Nectar-bearing compound flowers that are brightly colored, such as those in the daisy family—asters, marigolds, and zinnias. Old varieties, more like the wild original species, usually provide more nectar than highly hybridized and/or double flowers.
• Butterfly bushes: *Buddleia davidii* and *B. alternifolia*.
• Spring bloom such as lilacs, azaleas, and golden alyssum *Aurelia*.
• Late bloom such as goldenrods, gaillardia, blazing stars *(Liatris)*, and michaelmas daisies.
• Many herbs, especially hyssop, the sages, and catnip.
• A variety of flower colors, but favorites may be orange, pink, lavender, purple, yellow, and white.

Here are some tips on planning your butterfly garden:
• If possible, plant your flowers where they receive full sun for most of the day.
• If you raise vegetables, plant some butterfly-attracting flowers among the vegetables. The blooms add color and some of the flowers act as companion plants to vegetables, warding off some insects that might otherwise require pesticides. Some visiting butterflies are excellent garden-crop pollinators.
• To satisfy butterflies' entire life-cycle needs, you might try to provide food for them in their caterpillar phase: red clover or alfalfa for sulphur butterflies; parsley, dill, lovage, or fennel for the black swallowtail group; milkweeds for monarchs and queens.

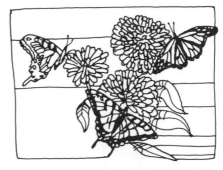

• To avoid a severe setback in your butterfly-gardening efforts, use chemical and biological pest controls sparingly, if at all.
• To draw the largest number of butterflies, plant flowers that will provide perpetual butterfly bloom from late March through early frosts.

Even when a gardener gets off to a fast start, butterfly gardens take time to build. Pages 42-45 explore other attractive ways and means to create a butterfly habitat.

A Trio of Painted Ladies

I still have a few neighbors who regard me with some suspicion. Perhaps my gardening efforts are a bit different. And when I shout down the block for the kids to come meet the painted ladies, more than my gardening idiosyncrasies are questioned.

The painted ladies whose visits I encourage are butterflies. Three kinds are common—the American painted lady east of the Rockies, the West Coast lady along the Pacific Coast, and the cosmopolite which ranges throughout North America.

The key to attracting painted ladies—as with other wildlife—is providing suitable habitat. Offer food, water, and places where their young can hide, and your chances of enticing them to your yard are excellent. Pesticides and butterflies don't mix, however, so if you use chemicals, do so with care.

The American painted lady is my favorite. Few designs in nature surpass the beauty and intricacy of its underside pattern. To encourage adults to visit, provide nectar sources such as tithonia and zinnias or plant native wildflowers such as mountain mint, dogbane, or goldenrod. If you plant leafy foods for the caterpillars, you can watch the entire life cycle of this splendid creature played out in your yard. Key larval foods include pussy toes, pearly everlasting, and rabbit tobacco. The attractively patterned caterpillars construct small leaf tents that get larger as the caterpillars eat and grow.

I've established a small carpet of pussy toes in the poor, dry soil of my front yard and the painted ladies have responded accordingly.

The cosmopolite is not nearly as dependable a visitor, and for good reason. It cannot tolerate freezing temperatures, so any of its kind remaining north in the fall simply freeze to death. Every spring, however, this butterfly erupts from its northern Mexican wintering grounds and moves north across the continent, laying eggs on dozens of species of plants. The cosmopolite's favorites include plants in the thistle group, the mallow family (including hollyhocks), and certain bean family plants. Thistle may be your best bet for bringing them to your yard.

The West Coast lady is not an acquaintance of mine, but gardeners should look for it on butterfly bush, lantanas, and native wildflowers. Its caterpillars feed almost exclusively on mallow family plants. To attract the West Coast lady, native plants such as the globemallows and sidalceas should be nurtured in a wildflower area and hollyhocks and rose of Sharon can be planted in more traditional gardens.

These butterflies are terrific additions to your circle of friends. Invite them to visit this summer!

I plant mystery in my small suburban patch of landscape, and more times than not, I am pleasantly surprised.

This year I interplanted scarlet annual phlox with Tribute strawberries along our front curb. I figured that I would get more color per square foot, and the phlox would encourage butterflies. The mixture worked well. I haven't figured out yet whether neighborhood kids see the combined red tones and dismiss both as flowers or see the flowers and then discover the joys of picking their own strawberries. Come to think of it, I have been offering an increasing number of strawberry picking lessons lately.

Zinnias, marigolds, impatiens, and buddleias can form the nucleus of a surefire butterfly-attracting garden. If you want to add more zing to your butterfly plantings, visit a nearby meadow, marsh, or scrub patch and learn which plants butterflies visit.

My wanderings have introduced me to six species of native wildflowers and shrubs which attract a wonderful variety of butterflies.

If skippers are the ever-present sparrows of the butterfly world, then hairstreaks are the more uncommon warbler equivalent. These intricately patterned small butterflies dart from perch to flower and back again. To identify them, you need to make them sit still long enough for you to examine them. As with children, the best way to keep them in one place is to feed them something they love to eat. For these butterflies, small white flowers in large clusters have the appeal of ice cream and cake to a child. Three native shrubs that do the job for me are buttonbush, sweet pepperbush, and New Jersey tea. A perennial wildflower, narrow-leaved mountain mint, is highly attractive to other butterflies as well.

One other flower that works wonders is shepherd's needle, a weedy southeastern roadside plant. If you aren't sure about its butterfly attractiveness, just count the number of butterflies shown sipping at this flower in *Butterflies East of the Great Plains* by Paul Opler and George Krizek. Use this white wildflower as an annual if you live out of its normal range.

A couple of yellow butterfly magnets, both found wild, are lance-leaved coreopsis, which blooms from April through August, and tickseed sunflower, which flowers July through September. Skippers find the coreopsis a favorite. The tickseed, *Bidens aristosa*, is a favorite of monarchs.

Numerous native-plant nurseries offer the shrubs I've mentioned. To grow the flowers, seek out the plants and collect their seeds. For shepherd's needle seed, plan a late February trip to scour Florida's roadsides. After all, what other reason could there be for a winter trip to Florida?

Milkweeds and Monarchs

The question of whether milkweeds are weeds or wildflowers shouldn't bother anyone. Who cares what they're called when they do so much for one's property?

Milkweeds attract butterflies as few other plants can. The sun-loving milkweeds add vibrant color, sturdy structure, and delightful fragrance to a midsummer garden. The sweet milkweed scent that draws so many butterflies adds a delightful surprise to a garden: the daytime aroma changes at dusk to a wonderful fragrance that's likely to bring in many moths.

From June through early September, butterflies of all varieties—from the small skippers to the largest swallowtails—search out milkweed nectar, which the plants produce copiously.

Throughout most of North America, milkweed is the monarch butterfly caterpillar's sole source of food, as well as the location of its nursery and the means of protection from enemies. Adult monarchs lay their eggs on the plants. When the young hatch, their entire food supply is at hand in milkweed leaves. A chemical in milkweed's milky sap, ingested by the young, protects both caterpillar and mature butterfly by making them distasteful to birds. That helps maintain butterfly populations against natural predation.

In the southern states, milkweeds attract queens, butterflies that are related to monarchs and need the same food and protection.

Most milkweeds thrive in well-drained soil that gets plenty of sun. Here are some kinds for your garden:

Common milkweed (*Asclepias syriaca*). This one displays pale, reddish pink, or pearl-colored flowers. The plant probably produces the most stems in the shortest time. It may spread like a weed, but it's pretty.

Butterfly weed (*A. tuberosa*) is sometimes called "pride of the meadow." A valued perennial and the prettiest of the milkweeds, it grows from a stout central root and will not spread, except by seed. Native orange forms range throughout the country, but yellows and reds may also be found.

Red milkweeds (*A. rubra* and *A. curassavica*). These are red and yellow species found along the Atlantic and Gulf coasts.

Swamp milkweed (*A. incarnata*). This one is a slow spreader. Its dusky pink flowers are highly attractive to butterflies, including virtually all of the swallowtails.

Garden centers and some mail-order firms carry some milkweeds. Other kinds are perhaps best acquired in the field. Identify the plants during their summer bloom; in late fall, harvest the seeds and hold them outdoors or in your refrigerator. In early spring, start the seeds outdoors, lightly covering them with good, well-drained soil. Then just sit back and watch the show: flowers, caterpillars, butterflies—all in a colorful progression.

A wildlife gardener is usually at the mercy of nature's mysterious cycles. Although I have planted carefully to attract monarch butterflies, they have not shown up in healthy numbers for the better part of two years. But beginning in mid-August, many female monarchs deposited eggs on my milkweeds. So many fresh adults are now gliding, prancing, and feeding throughout our meadow that I wonder what caused the turn-around in this beautiful butterfly's fortunes.

By late fall, the monarchs head south for the winter. Perhaps one in every thousand monarchs that I view will exit the United States alive. Fewer still will arrive safely at their overwintering ground in the Sierra Madre of Mexico. Late in the Mexican mountain winter, the remaining butterflies begin their return flight to our country. With luck, good weather, and a continuous milkweed supply, the monarchs will return and repopulate much of the United States.

Over the years, tantalizing evidence has suggested that other butterflies migrate as monarchs do, though over a shorter route and in lesser numbers. Research—and possibly the efforts of interested backyard gardeners across the country—will uncover more information on butterfly migration.

Many kinds of butterflies move north with the spring and never return to their place of birth. They mate farther and farther north with each brief generation, but two factors limit their conquest of northern lands: the lack of specific foods required by the caterpillars, and the fatally cold weather.

Some of our best known and most attractive butterflies are only seasonal visitors. Their lives parallel those of the many birds that race north out of Central and South America each spring. Buckeyes, red admirals, painted ladies, and variegated fritillaries are among the many species that follow this route. Despite fatalities in the North, these species return each summer.

Other southern emigrants may be truly rare in your area and are called, somewhat negatively, vagrants. In the western suburbs of Washington, D.C., where we make our home, more than 10 varieties of beautiful southern butterflies could possibly show up in my yard. I try to plant their favorite foods,

as I do for uncommon local species and for monarchs. The southward-bound monarchs prefer to feed on small white native asters, for instance.

Your chances of seeing unusual butterflies are greatly enhanced by planting lures of their favorite nectar foods and the native plants their caterpillars need as foods. Cultivating these uncommon native plant species boosts your chances of adding more species of butterflies to your Backyard Wildlife Habitat guest list.

Six-legged Singers

Now, in autumn's waning days, I listen intently to my backyard meadow for sounds of summer gone by. Fairly large by garden-plot standards, the meadow is more than just another planting bed. It lives flamboyantly. Its lives and the life supports that animate it are varied and wonderful: animals, plants, soil, sun, air, water.

I am saddened as this wildflower-riddled patch slips into the apparent stillness of winter. Attuned to its daily rhythms, I can't help but notice the diminution of its sound and motion.

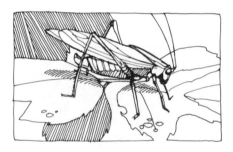

Indian summer has returned briefly today, however. Late afternoon sun stirs the remaining tree crickets and other long-horned grasshoppers. The day's heat dissipates slowly into a late evening chill. Later, as I finally nod off, I'm comforted by what might be the year's last chorus of katydids.

Insect song in late summer and fall is the equal of spring's more lauded orchestra of bird and frog song. Yet it is often overlooked. Perhaps by September we've had our fill of nature. Some of us fought losing battles with insects throughout the summer. We tune out their wonderful, autumnal chorus and go about our outdoor chores and hobbies oblivious to their lives.

Like birds, some insects use song to attract mates, defend territories, and warn of impending danger. The ma-

jority of these unseen songsters belong to the insect group *Orthoptera*. In addition to locusts, this group includes katydids, crickets, grasshoppers of all types, and walking sticks. All but the walking sticks are singers.

The astute human listener is able to grasp the diversity of life in a wild spot. With practice, I can now distinguish 20 different kinds of insect sound during the brief minutes between sunset and darkness. Daylight triggers songs from a quite different cast of performers.

Getting to know these critters is harder than learning about birds. Listen for a frequently repeated song. Track that sound to its source by slowly approaching the singer. Although you may not find your songster in any field guide, you might jot down notes about its appearance. Some species seem to be adept ventriloquists. If you become totally frustrated in your search for the insect itself, try to find a copy of the record album, *The Sounds of Insects,* produced years ago by Houghton Mifflin Co. If that search is successful, try to identify your insect.

Recognizing and appreciating some of these smaller but no less important species of wildlife in your yard might change your view of wildlife entirely. And just think what a conversation starter your description of the mating call of the sword-bearing conehead or tinkling ground cricket might be at your next social gathering.

No matter where you live—near the mountains of New England, the deserts of Arizona, or the rain forests of Washington—you'll find fascinating little creatures that biologists call isopods.

Any backyard treasure hunt will probably turn up isopods: what the treasure hunters may call wood lice, roly-polys, sow bugs, or pill bugs. They're found where it's damp, invariably *under* things: rocks, rotting leaves, boards, bricks, or in the deep, rich soil of a compost pile.

Making a rockpile habitat for isopods and other small animals in your yard can prove to be just as satisfying as providing a nest box for bluebirds.

The land-dwelling crustaceans are relatives of lobster, shrimp, and crabs. They breathe through gills, so they need extra moisture to live. Most isopods are pale grey, but sometimes you'll find a white one that has just molted and is briefly wearing a "soft shell" (just like a molting crab does).

Isopods are harmless and can become a source of endless wonder. Touch a roly-poly or pill bug and it may roll up into a little ball. Rolled up, its soft underbelly is protected from attack by predators such as spiders and ants. Rolling up also blocks out air that can suffocate the small creature by drying out its gills.

In your backyard, isopods function much as earthworms do—chewing up rotting or injured plant material and enriching the soil with their excretions. Some isopods feed on other isopods and other small animals. One kind of isopod lives its whole life in ant nests, eating ant larvae.

When an isopod eats, it holds its food with the front pair or two of its seven pairs of legs. It can walk fast. The steps of one ocean-side kind of isopod have actually been counted: 16 steps per second—per foot. With all 14 feet going at once, a single isopod may plant 224 footsteps each second—a real thundering herd!

Isopods see poorly and "smell" with their antennae. Because of their need for moisture, they have sensitive, humidity-seeking scanners. They also are equipped with uropods—two tail-like projections at the end of their bodies. Some isopods can form a tube with their uropods to pick up water and

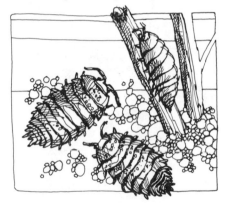

send it to their gills. Special rear-end glands can spray noxious chemicals at enemies intent on an isopod meal. The spray is harmless to people.

Isopod young are born somewhat in the manner of crabs and somewhat like kangaroos. Eggs hatch in a pouch (marsupium) filled with fluid. From 10 to 50 isopods develop in this aqueous nursery until they're ready to pop out and crawl away, just like isopods have been doing for millions of years.

Owls: Harbingers of Spring

While we humans may feel no hint of spring in the winter air, invisible hormonal changes are taking place within many plants and animals as their internal clocks synchronize with the imperceptibly lengthening days.

The first signs of spring come earlier than the return of robins or even the bursting into bloom of hazelnut. In late December, spring activities crank up among two species of owls: the great horned owl and the barred owl.

The great horned owl, the larger of the two, starts setting up its nesting territories by Christmas. That's a great time to listen for the hooting of pairs. Horned owls will be sitting on eggs come early February, even in the coldest part of their nesting range.

Some ice-crystal-clear morning at 5:00 a.m., just sit on a hilltop and listen for the great horned owls, each pair guarding acres and acres of woodlands. The deeper hoot of the male responds to the more mellow alto hoot of the female. Sometimes several pairs of owls will call to each other.

These raptors prey mainly on small mammals and birds, but legends about the variety of their prey abound. Small house cats, skunks, even young peregrine falcons are fair game. But like most birds, owls are more feathers than body, and can't fly off with prey that weighs more than they do.

Young great horneds are often feeding at the nest by late February and frequently leave the nest while still flightless. At that stage they're known as "branchers," making their way from tree to tree by hopping and flapping. I once monitored a great horned owl nest in coastal New Jersey for the entire nesting season. During the six- to eight-week incubation and fledgling period, I was surprised to find very freshly-caught flounder (among various foods) at the base of the tree.

The barred owl, slightly smaller than the great horned, seems to prefer stream bottoms and woodlands, and may be more wary of suburbia than the great horned is. It does not have the great horned's ear tufts. Nevertheless, its hearing and night vision are acute, and it, too, is an aggressive predator.

Barred owls tend to nest later in the season than the great horned. Great horned owls invariably take over nests built by crows or hawks. Barred owls are more likely to take up residence in a hollow tree or a nest box.

A box in your yard won't guarantee a nesting owl, but you can always listen for a barred owl on cold winter nights. Its hoot (often paraphrased as "Who cooks for you?") is similar to the call of a great horned ("hoot") owl. But some of its other vocalizations, including what might be described as maniacal laughter, may be enough to wake *you* from winter doldrums.

Chapter Five

It's a Jungle Out There

When insects invade a treasured garden, many gardeners automatically will arm themselves for the "battle with the bugs." On go the masks and gloves; out come the swatters, spray-guns, and dusters. The summer-long war is on.

Yet such tactics usually produce only Pyrrhic victories: the pests are destroyed all right, but in the process, "good" insects die with them. At the same time the insecticides drench the whole garden with poisons.

Left alone, nature can often handle the "bad" bugs, needing help only when a pest onslaught is severe.

Many predatory insects ("good" bugs) make up nature's "hit" squads against insect pests. Dozens of helpful insects eat other insects and you can, with care, enlist the help of these "good bugs" in your own yard.

Mantids. Often called "praying mantises," these helpful relatives of grasshoppers are not the pests their cousins are. Their appetite for insects is voracious. You can buy mantid eggs, or you can get them for free by collecting the eggs from a field. In the winter, look along the stems of shrubs and wildflowers for elongated or globular egg masses, which have the color and texture of dirty white plastic foam. Then just place the egg mass, with twig attached, in your backyard to hatch in the spring.

Ladybird beetles. These little yellow, orange, or red beetles are commonly seen throughout most of North America. Both adults and larvae eat pests such as aphids. "Ladybugs" are apt to show up on their own. But beetles can also be bought through mail order seed catalogs.

Wasps. Many people can't abide wasps (large or small or any color), but to any gardener not allergic to stings, wasps can be valuable allies. Large common paper wasps, which go by the scientific name of *Polistes*, go for caterpillars in a big way and are actually one of the gentlest of large wasps. (Hornets, yellow jackets, and other paper wasps are much fiercer, and most homeowners can't tolerate them at all.) Tiny, parasitic wasps (which can be purchased) lay their eggs on insect pests. Some wasps pollinate fruit and vegetable plants, assuring good crops.

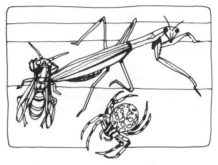

Spiders. Although spiders are not insects, they do help control insect pests. When you see large, beautiful, well-constructed webs, don't destroy them. The spiders that spin these webs prey on moths, crickets, and grasshoppers and feed mostly at night.

Predatory insects, like many animals, are territorial—they stake out their own spaces to rule. So don't overload your garden with one kind of insect-ally. Many will simply starve, leave the garden, or eat each other up. Just enough predators keep pests at bay—without spraying.

Insects—Friends and Foes

To most people, fall means an end to insects. Well, yes and no. They may not be crawling or flying around, but insect friends and foes are still there—in our yards; out in the meadows, fields, and woods; or in masses of eggs.

My kids and I look forward to our annual fall insect hunt, when we keep a lookout for insect egg masses. The eggs of problem insects we destroy; those of beneficial insects we try to protect. You can do the same.

Arm yourself with good books so that you'll recognize one insect or egg mass from another. Such guides are available from your state forestry department or the United States Department of Agriculture. You can also consult *The Golden Guide to the Insects* or *The Book on Garden Insect Pests.* Here's what you might find:

INSECT PESTS

Gypsy moths, which have invaded much of the northeastern and north central United States, hatch in spring and devour leaves. Look along tree trunks, under picnic tables, and in woodpiles for the eggs (usually a dirty brown mass 1 1/2 to 2 inches long and almost as wide). Remove and destroy.

Bag worm caterpillars can defoliate and kill many kinds of trees and shrubs in the spring, especially junipers and arborvitae. Cut their egg bags, constructed of plant debris and silk, off branches with scissors and throw the bags away. You can also spray the caterpillars themselves in the spring. Use only BT (available under a variety of trade names); it's a bacterial insecticide specifically for moth and butterfly *caterpillars* that's harmless to other forms of wildlife—and to you.

Eastern tent caterpillars are visible in many eastern states from late March into mid-June. Their unsightly, squirming silk tents festoon wild black cherry and related trees. However, even defoliated trees can recover, and certain birds (notably the cuckoos) prey on the caterpillars. You *might* tolerate them. If you choose not to, look for very small, shiny egg clumps resembling varnished foam. Break up the clump. You can also break up tents in the spring or spray the feeding caterpillars with BT. Don't burn them; you'll only damage the tree or shrub.

BENEFICIAL INSECTS

Mantises are voracious eaters of insect pests in the spring. You might find their patterned egg masses attached to the stems of shrubs (which can be left alone) or to annual wildflower stems (which you can bring home to your garden). The egg masses are longer than they are wide and look like dirty cotton.

Lady bird beetles (often called "ladybugs") avidly eat aphids in the spring. If you're in luck you'll find them right in your yard, hibernating in woodpiles or rock piles. Wherever you find them, gently return their covering, and even add some leaf mulch to protect them until spring.

When you've created an inviting backyard habitat, you expect wild creatures to make themselves naturally at home. Being "at home," however, can mean that wild animals behave more "naturally" than you may have bargained for. You may not have anticipated that your friendly birds, furry beasts, and busy bugs were going to turn your yard into something of a jungle.

That's what shocked my own four-year-old, Dan, one morning last spring. He innocently looked out into our yard, a wildlife habitat certified by the National Wildlife Federation, a "place of refuge" for all kinds of wild animals. And what did he see? Several robins munching on the earthworms he and I had been carefully nurturing! We had been trying to turn our clay-based ground into organic-rich soil. Young Dan had become fond of the earthworms and guarded them as zealously as a sow bear guards her cubs. When he saw those birds after "his" worms, the robins became "mean" and he beat on the sliding glass door to scare the "worm-killers" away.

The robins, of course, were just doing what comes naturally. Dan's a bit young to understand that the robins wouldn't eat *all* the worms, and that we wanted both earthworms *and* robins in our backyard.

You, like Dan, may feel angry at the sight of one animal killing its "victim." But there's really no way around it: if you have prey, you'll have predators. This is a natural process, but you can take steps to control predation—at least in your own yard.

It's a minor challenge to control the predation of skunks, raccoons, opossums, some squirrels, and such exciting visitors as woodland hawks. Provide dense evergreen and spiny-shrub cover for wildlife prey to hide in. Keep food unavailable to predators that also scavenge (tight lids on trash cans, etc.). Put your nesting boxes on poles and attach baffles below them. Baffles may also keep snakes (the ones that climb) from getting to the nests.

You can bell your own cat, and keep it indoors at dawn and dusk (when wildlife is most active). To deter neighborhood cats, place your bird feeders where the cats cannot lurk below them. Feral cats (house cats gone wild) should be humanely trapped and removed by properly trained persons.

Your community leash laws provide you with a tool for the control of runaway dogs. Dogs are usually less troublesome to wildlife than cats, but both will go after birds (cats especially chase

young birds), shrews, moles, and rabbits. In reality, however, many wild animals get so used to the habits of domestic animals that they are able to avoid them.

Take precautions to diffuse the predation in your backyard, but remember: a natural food web includes predator/prey relationships. There is no need to be *too* dismayed (as Dan was) when a robin grabs a worm.

Tolerating Yellowjackets?

With the first frost just days away, I started the mower and headed toward the 8-inch-high grass near the yellow-jacket nest. Throughout the summer, a city of *Vespula maculifrons*, a common yellowjacket wasp, had bustled under the branches of a young hornbeam tree. From the safe vantage point of my deck, I had just seen that their community life was a shambles, their organization in disarray. My mowing went successfully and yielded the desired results—short grass and no stings.

I had considered the alternative—to spray with an insecticide and mow earlier. The yellowjackets' inconspicuous nest site, my inertia, and some understanding had spared their colony.

Yellowjackets belong to the highly social group of insects known as paper wasps, and they are among the most feared of all backyard wildlife. One step too close to an active nest can launch dozens of formidably armed worker wasps on a collision course with your entire anatomy. Why even think of tolerating them for a moment?

The first time I watched a yellowjacket seize and eat a striped cucumber beetle was two years ago. Until recently, I could not successfully grow cucumbers because of the bacterial wilt that these beetles spread. This year, we had few striped beetles—we saw yellowjackets eating them. Coincidence or not, we maintained a tenuous peace with these ground-nesting wasps and enjoyed a bountiful cucumber harvest.

Perhaps you've vied with yellowjackets over a hamburger at a late summer picnic. These wasps, unlike most adult wasps, enjoy a high protein diet. This same appetite is characteristic of their larvae.

At times, nature controls these creatures. But sometimes human intervention is necessary. Insecticides designed to kill wasps and hornets are sold at garden centers and hardware stores. To maximize their effectiveness and minimize your chances of being stung, spray during the night when all of the wasps are at home and are lethargic due to cooler temperatures.

If you choose not to spray, the best way to avoid being stung is to stay away from the nest. If you want to destroy the nest, alternatives to spraying include trapping—more effective in the western states than in the East—or vacuuming insects at the nest site with a shop vacuum cleaner at night. An unproven but interesting suggestion to rid your yard of nests involves pouring honey around the nest entrance. The honey attracts skunks which eat both the honey and subterranean yellowjackets—workers, queen, and larvae. For some people, skunks are no more welcome than wasps. And if skunks don't roam your neighborhood, you would only wind up with sticky, well-fed yellowjackets.

A year ago, my sons spotted what appeared to be the black soaker hose slithering around the grape trellis and heading for the vegetable garden. The 6-foot-long black rat snake that they understandably mistook for the hose didn't stay in the yard for long, but its visit was cause for wonder, some anxiety, and dozens of questions for weeks to come. In a Backyard Wildlife Habitat, the first visit by any new animal neighbor is a proclamation that your hard labor has paid off. Mother Nature need not be relegated solely to national parks and wildlife refuges.

In the eastern United States, the black rat snake is generally the largest snake and is also commonly seen. Its length (up to 8 feet) is impressive. Its ability to climb trees is always somewhat disconcerting. A 7-foot snake ascending an oak gives your yard that aura of Amazonia that even high humidity and temperatures in the nineties cannot duplicate.

Like many large snakes, the black rat is a constrictor, a squeezer of its prey. On farms and in feed lots, its diet includes rats and mice. In suburbia, rabbits, chipmunks, and birds fuel its growth.

These snakes are active from the last spring frost to the first one of fall. In winter, most rat snakes in a given geographic area hibernate together.

Snakes don't respond as directly as songbirds to efforts to attract them. You can't find a snake feeder at your garden center, but you can modify your property to encourage snakes and many other kinds of inoffensive but misunderstood animals to visit.

Dense foliage close to the ground offers feeding and hiding areas. Exposed bedrock, stone walls, or rock piles provide places to overwinter, bask in the sun, search for food, and escape from predators.

Many of us apply a thick layer of bark mulch to our planting beds. This is the ideal place for a female black rat snake to lay a clutch of 20 to 30 eggs. Upon hatching in late summer, the attractively patterned black and light gray young remain in the cozy mulch for weeks before venturing away from their nursery in search of insects and frogs.

If you reside in an area where there are many venomous snakes, you may want to eliminate log and rock piles and other habitat that attracts snakes. Should you wish to have songbirds nesting on your property, then attracting black rat snakes will of course be counterproductive.

My family enjoys the occasional snakes we see as well as families of rabbits and bluebirds. Yes, our snake visitors dine on other residents but that's what happens in the suburban outback. For us, it's enlightening to have the outback on the back steps. What others might view as disturbing, we take in as the next chapter in a story that just never ends.

Lizard Visitors

Garden for lizards? Absolutely. Once you've seen a lizard do a "push-up," you'll want more around. And, as a welcome benefit, lizards make themselves useful by eating insects.

One of my most vivid childhood memories is the day I discovered an eastern fence lizard in a dead pine tree near my New Jersey home. Moving against the bark, looking for ants and other insects, the lizard was hard to see at first.

But watching lizards can be as entertaining and educational as watching birds and butterflies. When a lizard does "push-ups," it is really just bobbing its head several times in rapid succession; then it moves to another spot and repeats the performance. It's the lizard's way of marking its territory.

Being cold-blooded creatures, most lizards enjoy a sunny environment; they prefer temperatures between 80 and 100 degrees. They're attracted to wood or brush piles or stone and masonry walls—places that absorb heat and hold it. Here they can bask, wait for insects to fly or crawl by, take quick cover when danger appears, or if egg-layers, lay their eggs, usually leaving them to hatch without parental care.

All small lizards are harmless to humans. Initially, you may have to introduce lizards to your enhanced environment, but then they'll stay. Here are some common garden lizards:

Spiny lizards (also known in the East as fence or scrub lizards) lay one batch of two to five eggs per year in loose soil within their living area. They are often attractively camouflaged with collars, blotches, and specks contrasting with their background color.

Whiptail lizards are generally slimmer than fence lizards. Their patterns are brighter (often in green, black, and white stripes) and they have wider food preferences than do fence lizards. In South America, I've watched them eat garbage. In the United States, they can be found in much of the southern half of the country.

Geckos, a more southern lizard group, are, like spiny lizards, patterned for bark or stone camouflage. Their flat bodies and toe disks are distinctive. Look for them as they walk up walls, rocks, and tree trunks, prowling for insects and spiders.

Skinks may live farther north in the United States than any other lizards do. They're rarely seen in the open, but you'll hear them among dry leaves or in brush piles. Skinks may have two distinctive features: electric blue tails (seen only on juveniles in most species) and weak legs. When frightened they may slither away like snakes.

You may be able to train any of these lizards to visit a feeding area for scraps of meat or meal worms. And nearby, they'll be comfortable in the warm, safe rock or brush piles you've constructed for them.

Most of us recall the hallmarks in the development of our garden: the picking of the first home-grown apple or perhaps the year that we bested the neighbors by producing the very first vine-ripe tomato. Wildlife gardeners, however, remember other hallmarks: sighting the first hummingbird to visit the beebalm or discovering a golden-flecked chrysalis of a monarch butterfly on a flower stem.

I experienced one such hallmark this Memorial Day. I celebrated the arrival of the first mole to visit my yard. Most gardeners regard the visit of a mole as highly undesirable. Such celebration is akin to welcoming a gypsy moth caterpillar to a favorite oak tree.

Six or seven kinds of tunneling mammals known as moles can be found throughout much of the United States. In the eastern states, three species of moles make their homes; four species live in the Northwest.

Moles spend most of their lives underground, where they busily dig tunnels, raise their young, and dine on earthworms, insect larvae, and other small critters that live beneath our feet.

Why was I joyful about our mole visitor? For one, I had never watched a mole tunneling before. Memorial Day morning was warm. Waking early, I put out the flag and glanced at a nearby bark-mulched bed that is but a year old. The bark mulch was quaking. The mole below me was looking for breakfast. I invited my entire family out to relish this earthshaking event.

After watching the mole tunnel away from us, I grabbed a sharp spade, and, charting the mole's direction, placed the shovel behind the mole and dug it up. Placing soil and mole in a bucket, I carried the bucket to a nearby natural area and released the animal.

I enjoyed observing a creature I had never seen in operation before. Also, the mole indicated to me that I had developed good, rich soil inhabited by a tasty variety of mole appetizers. A true gardening triumph!

Many gardeners wish to control moles. The moles, probably not more than 5 inches long, do make holes and tunnels in the yard.

The most effective manner of controlling them is the procedure that I used. If you see a mole tunneling through your yard, simply grab your shovel and dig up the mole. Put it into a bucket, and release it in suitable mole habitat away from your yard.

By eliminating one or two moles, you can be mole-free for a good while. If you can't spend the time watching and digging for them, you can use traps to kill them.

But rather than running for the mole trap, try to tolerate the mole or remove it live and release it in suitable habitat. When a mole appears in *your* yard, think about the visitor that made that tunnel. Moles indicate good soil and, perhaps, good wildlife habitat.

Dealing with Groundhogs

The first frost has touched the tops of the peppers and eggplants, marking the end of another summer of gardening. Last night I frantically gathered all of the okra pods fit to eat and all of the ripening tomatoes.

With some regrets I note the passing of the season, yet this time of year has always brought a sigh of relief. It means the end of the battle with groundhogs, which may now give us gardeners a respite for the winter.

I have sometimes believed that groundhogs are something of a family curse. I came to Virginia from New Jersey. Mom still lives in New Jersey. She

has groundhogs. Brother Bob, who lives down the street from Mom—he's got groundhogs, too. Mom has given up vegetable gardening and no longer battles her groundhogs. But Bob periodically rages at these gargantuan tunnelers, and he makes inroads on their population so that his family can enjoy home-grown tomatoes.

Groundhogs (or woodchucks) are the world's largest squirrel. Zoologists lodge *Marmota monax* right in with tree squirrels and prairie dogs, all members of the *Sciuridae* family.

Phenomenal diggers, groundhogs usually forage close to their underground labyrinth but are perfectly capable of climbing trees to get food or to escape from enemies. These short-tailed critters may weigh up to 14 pounds. I hope one never falls out of a tree as I walk below.

Groundhogs range throughout the eastern United States, into the Midwest and across much of Canada. They graze mostly on grasses and wildflowers. If their home is in the suburbs, however, they snack voraciously on our beans, marigolds, cantaloupes, other succulent morsels, and yes—tomatoes.

One way to try to outwit a groundhog is to fence it out. Around the perimeter of your garden, dig heavy-duty galvanized fencing 2 feet in the ground, with 6-8 more inches of fence angling out and down from the 2-foot mark. Then bury the fence.

In my own yard, I've put all my vegetables in raised beds constructed of pressure-treated lumber. It's easy to fence such a garden because the posts that anchor the lumber also anchor the fence. Although a groundhog may try going underneath, in this case my absolutely miserable, clayey, rocky soil is a blessing. Groundhogs are no more willing to tunnel through it than they are through concrete.

Actually, I can't complain this year. Groundhogs have rarely attempted to enter my garden, nor have they bothered my unfenced plants. I think perhaps they have found enough food in the clovers, evening primroses, and succulent grasses of my natural meadow garden nearby. At any rate they have done no real damage, and I'm beginning to believe I've discovered a couple of cures for the family curse.

The Tomato Bandit

Dan, our six-year-old gardener, came running into the house one morning last June, big tears streaming down his cheeks. His first cherry tomato of the year, ripe on a bush he had carefully tended all spring, had been nibbled on by a sloppy eater who hadn't even had the courtesy to remove the now tarnished prize from the plant. A tomato poacher was loose in our yard!

After Dan's anger subsided, we plotted a strategy to identify the culprit. Each morning, Dan made an early visit to the plant, removed any partially eaten tomatoes, and searched for the tomato bandit.

On the fourth day, the morning dawned blisteringly hot, with not a wisp of breeze stirring the trees. Yet from our vantage point in the family room, we saw the tomato plant quake. Dan slipped out the back door and stalked the intruder. As he neared, the tomato plant stopped shaking. Dan closed in, pounced . . . and lifted the culprit high for us to see. The tomato poacher was a box turtle.

Box turtles, small land turtles that range over much of the United States east of the Rockies, prefer a mix of habitat: meadow and lawn, some scrubby tangles of undergrowth, and perhaps a patch of woodland. Such places often abound in new developments, parklands, and stream corridors.

Turtles' habits cause no real damage to the plants we grow. Box turtles usually endear themselves to children of all ages and are one of the most visible wildlife species in the country.

But sadly, box turtles are on the decline; in many areas they are truly rare. Box turtles, it seems, have irreconcilable problems with our lifestyles. Have you ever seen a turtle sprint out of the way of speeding vehicles? Have you watched one jump out of a swimming pool, culvert, or storm sewer?

Perhaps we need a national campaign to help the box turtles. You can run your own campaign by trying to retain a mix of habitats in your community. You can stop your car safely off the road and assist box turtles out of the road and into nearby woods.

Fences that reach the ground turn into turtle roadblocks. If your yard is fenced, one or two openings, 5 inches high by 6 inches wide, will allow entry and exit for the turtles.

Cherry tomatoes and strawberries, grown on the edge of planting beds, are ideal turtle foods. You can plant some for yourself and some for the turtles (that's what we decided to do). Brush piles or mounds of wood chips provide areas for them to overwinter and to lay their eggs. Dense, shading shrubbery offers resting and feeding habitat. You needn't do more than that as a turtle gardener.

In my neighborhood, turtles still run free. Kids say that they're the best wildlife "show and tell" on the block. That's reason enough for me to lend a box turtle a hand whenever I can.

Dealing with Toxic Trash

Once in a great while, spurred by comments from family members, I am overcome by the urge to clean up the garage. There are dangers out there. My 11-year-old son recently tried to pry his bicycle out of the garage but instead unleashed a cascade of tomato cages. In dodging that, he got entangled in drip irrigation tubing.

Cleanup progressed well until I uncovered four bottles of insecticides that I no longer use. My substitutes for these commonly used chemicals don't eliminate every last pest, but we've learned to accept a few blemishes, and our yard is full of life.

What kept me from completing my task was serious concern about following label directions for disposal of these now unwanted insecticides. No matter how toxic the chemical, with warnings such as "never spray near open water," or "toxic to fish and wildlife," I was directed to simply "wrap and place in trash collection."

Trash collection in our county proceeds like this: place your trash on the curb in the morning and by the end of the day, it's gone. It never really disappears, though. By the time it is buried at the landfill, the pesticide container has probably broken.

When a landfill leaks, and some do, or when such chemicals are disposed of improperly, they seep into the environment, polluting both ground and surface water. One way or another, we get our throwaways back—toxics in our drinking water, fish with contaminant levels making them unfit for consumption, or perhaps the elimination of all life from a local pond or stream.

I live in an area that does not provide me with a disposal alternative. Some counties, and even a progressive state or two, give their citizens the opportunity to dispose of these leftovers responsibly. Fairfax County, Virginia sponsors two household toxics round-ups each year. Homeowners bring their chemicals to specified locations and can feel confident that proper disposal will occur.

Maine, a state that has taken the bull by the horns, has established a container return program for agricultural users of pesticides. It also has conducted a limited number of pickups of household toxics.

On the scale of total pesticide use for the United States, the amount the homeowner uses may be small. Remember, however, that flushing a half quart of some readily available insecticide down a storm sewer could mean death for hundreds of species of tiny aquatic animals in a small pond half a mile away from your home.

The resilience of our wildlife species is incredible. But we need to remain vigilant about the quality of the environment we live in, and that concern can begin on your street. If you think safer pesticide disposal methods are needed in your community, make a few phone calls and find out what you can do to change the system. For the sake of my kids and the wildlife around me, I know that I will.

Chapter Six

Wooing Wildlife With Water, Flowers, and Shelter

If you remember your favorite childhood haunts, you undoubtedly recall the magic of small streams, tiny ponds, and intermittent rivulets.

The streams of our neighborhood were where my brother, other neighborhood children and I exercised our fledgling engineering skills. We built a new Panama Canal—in New Jersey. We sailed homemade boats. And we pretended to be beavers. We built dams. We created places where frogs and tadpoles could live.

Small streams are the favorite play habitat of children. That's what Lisa Schicker, a recent landscape architecture graduate of North Carolina State University, found in a two-year study of the ways children relate to their outdoor environment.

That's a hunch I've long had as an environmental educator. Here at the National Wildlife Federation's Laurel Ridge Education Center, where I work, kids who visit love to get in a stream, under parental supervision, and turn over rocks, searching for crayfish and other creepy-crawlies.

Neighborhood small streams are potentially the richest of all environments for suburban wildlife. In building our suburban developments, we must protect these small streams and a bit of the plant-clothed corridor that they weave through.

Corridors 100 feet or more wide may allow a variety of plant life to thrive. Animal life—everything from migrant songbirds and toads to opossums and foxes—moves in and out of this environment.

Rains may flush lawn fertilizers and pesticides out of our properties. Yet green corridors flanking a stream can keep the chemicals from getting into the stream system and polluting rivers and lakes. Excess fertilizers are taken up by the hardy native plants growing in the corridors.

As fields and forestlands have given way to residential development, most small streams have been eliminated, channeled, or placed in cement sluiceways or culverts. However, progressive developers have realized the value of preserving as much of the natural ecosystem as possible. Retaining open space not only enhances homesites

and provides a rich wildlife environment, it also allows a builder to command higher home prices.

It makes sense for homebuyers to pay the extra price to locate along stream corridors. Such property values are well protected—along with the corridor wildlife.

Suburban children benefit substantially from growing up in a rich natural environment. Through play in natural environments, kids develop ecological values early in life. They are far more apt than other children to become environmentally sensitive adults—with wonderful childhood memories, like yours and mine.

Birdbaths Woo Wildlife

Wild animals have simple needs: food, shelter—and water. For some reason many wildlife lovers faithfully provide food and shelter (seed, birdhouses, suet, and evergreens) but forget the easiest service: the supply of water. Perhaps they sincerely believe that animals naturally find ponds and streams to drink from and bathe in. But in most urban and suburban areas, few such natural water sources exist.

Since water is as vital to wildlife as it is to human life, providing a water source close to home is one sure-fire way to draw wildlife to your yard. For the moment, let's bypass the more complicated water provisions (ponds, pools, and fountains) and talk about the simplest source—*birdbaths*.

Any clean, shallow container will do—from a 1/2-inch deep, 6- to 8-inch wide saucer (such as a flower pot base) to a traditional 2- to 2 1/2-foot pedestal-mounted birdbath (light enough in weight to be easily tilted to clean). Fill it with plain tap water (no additives, please!). Since it's useful for both drinking and bathing, keep it clean, hosing it with a pressure nozzle and/or using a small scrub brush every two or three days.

What kind of wildlife will be drawn to your water? Mostly birds, but also squirrels and, in some areas, raccoons, opossums, groundhogs, chipmunks, and other mammals that come mainly to drink. Butterflies come to perch on the edge for a drink; frogs climb in and sit for awhile.

Visitation partly depends on where the water supply is placed. Water set right on the ground probably attracts the greatest variety of wildlife. It also has the advantages of being easy to clean and unlikely to break or tip over under the weight of heavier animals.

Providing water through the winter presents special problems (see page 66 for tips on how to do it).

If one birdbath can make *some* wildlife feel welcome, think of what several different kinds of birdbaths can draw to your yard! The birds may particularly enjoy a dip in a bath mounted on a pedestal. Place it in the sun near protecting foliage (for escape in case a predator shows up). The toad will probably opt for a bath set in the flower bed or in the shade of low ground cover. Wary animals such as the chipmunk may take advantage of a water source only if it's well-concealed in shrubbery. Besides serving wildlife well, a variety of birdbaths dotting your landscape adds to your own daily viewing pleasure.

How do birds choose a home? Much the same way you or I do. They evaluate, in their terms, all the important factors: Is the area attractive? Is it close to work (the finding of berries, insects, seeds, water)? Is the site good for a home? If there's already a home on the site, is it suitable? And, especially, is this a good place to raise a family?

Few things enhance a homeowner's enjoyment and understanding of life more than watching birds raise their young. And nothing makes watching easier than providing a birdhouse the birds can call their own. Wrens, chickadees, titmice, bluebirds, and swallows are prime occupants for ready-made homes which you can provide.

Your immediate surroundings will help you determine what kind of birds to provide for, if you want them close by. Chickadees and titmice like to nest in patches of large trees. Wrens are attracted to birdhouses placed among dense trees and shrubs, fairly close to the ground. Bluebirds opt for wide open spaces—extensive lawns, cemeteries, pastures, and even golf courses. Swallows like the same kind of open spaces—so long as they're close to rivers and ponds.

Each kind of bird is almost as choosy about the construction of its birdhouse as it is about its site. However, all the birds mentioned will move into a basic rectangular box, 5 inches wide by 10 inches high, built of unpainted, 1/2-inch spruce, fir, pine, or exterior plywood. The box should be equipped with 3/8-inch drainage holes in the bottom and a 1 1/2-inch entrance hole near the top of one side. Perches aren't needed and in fact may attract nesters such as house sparrows, which may injure the very wrens and chickadees

which you are trying to encourage to use the box.

Late winter or early spring is ideal birdhouse-building time. Mount the box 3 to 5 feet off the ground on a pole, fence post, or tree trunk.

Once a bird family has taken up residence, keep a close watch—for practical as well as pleasurable reasons. A day or two after the young leave the nest, it's birdhouse-cleaning time. If you have played host to bluebirds or wrens, chances are the parents will return to their cleaned-up home to raise a second brood in the same summer.

Winter Water for Wildlife

It's winter and it's difficult for wildlife to find water. Put yourself in the place of your friendly blue jay or gray squirrel: all their familiar watering sites are frozen or hidden beneath snow; the summer leaves that furnish water for small songbirds are gone.

Active winter creatures need water as much in winter as they do in summer, in part because of the stress of coping with the weather and a scarce food and water supply.

That's where you come in, but it's not easy. Winter birdbaths not only freeze, they get dirty faster than summer ones. Why? Winter users are apt to outnumber summer bathers, which usually come one by one. In winter, on the other hand, whole flocks descend

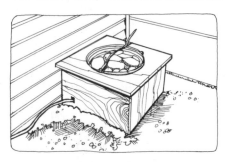

on your water supply. *One* flock of robins can leave a dirty birdbath behind. Also, the most frequent winter visitors are fruit-eating birds, notorious for their messy droppings.

Frequent ice-breaking and cleaning are therefore inevitable. But there are a few ways to save steps:

• Place your birdbath close enough to the house so that your chores (including lugging water buckets because outside faucets are turned off for the winter) are easier.

• To capture as much warmth as possible from the winter sun, site your birdbath on the south side of the house. If you can tuck the bath to leeward of dense, windshielding shrubbery, all the better.

• Stick a livestock watering-trough heater in a large birdbath. Thermostatically controlled, it keeps the water at about 35 degrees Farenheit, without running up your electrical bill or boiling the birds. (Always use proper *outdoor* extension cords.)

• Buy a birdbath with a built-in thermostatic heating coil (check catalogs from bird-feeding stores).

• You might try painting the interior of your birdbath with black exterior latex paint. Friends of mine tell me this turns it into a solar collector that warms the water. (I haven't tried this one myself.)

• Build a toasty bird-sauna such as the one designed by Harv and Robin Cashion, members of the National Wildlife Federation's Backyard Wildlife Habitat Program: take a 6- to 10-inch-deep galvanized pan with a 2- to 2 1/2-foot diameter. Wrap some thermostatic heating tape around the outside. Place rocks inside the pan, with some 2 inches below the top and some sticking above the top, thereby providing different depths of water for bathing and drinking. Plug the heating tape into an outdoor extension cord. Fill the pan with water and set it snugly into a stained wooden frame.

With this set-up you never have to de-ice. Just watch the birds splash in their warm sauna, and clean up once in a while after your guests.

Did you ever stop to think how much water rolls off your roof each year? If you live in Tucson, the quantity might be small. Where I live, though, summer thunderstorms and winter snows drop 40 inches of precipitation a year.

The system directing water off roofs is simple. Rain runs down the roof, follows the gutter to the downspout and streams across the ground. Much of this runoff (with its accumulated stock of motor oil, cigarettes, pesticides, and pet wastes from street gutters) then enters our local storm sewers.

Some minor calculations indicated that just half of the runoff from my roof could supply me with 14,000 gallons of water a year. I reasoned that I could direct the water in a more useful way. That quantity could fill a big fish tank or moisten a nifty little marsh. Someday, I'll live next to a marsh. Meanwhile, I'm enjoying one that I've built in my yard. I pronounced the marsh a success when butterflies began "mudpuddling" in droves on the moist soil.

My marsh project began to take shape in early winter. Step one was to outline the perimeter of the proposed marsh. My marsh is irregular in outline. This is due more to encounters with bedrock than to my sense of design. I stripped sod from a 450 square foot area, then excavated the subsoil and rock to about 14 inches deep.

I connected a downspout from our roof to a length of flexible plastic pipe. This I angled down and away from the house so that water would enter the top of the marsh. The next rainstorm, however, proved that the pipe angle was less than was needed and that my fill material was too porous. In April, I dug out the pipe, excavated the ditch with a greater angle, backfilled with clay, and thus slowed the overactive sump pump in my basement.

Next, I prepared a soil mixture that contained some sand, a dozen buckets of compost, a good quantity of the original subsoil and as much peat as I could afford. The marsh soil was mixed in place with my tough little rototiller. Areas of differing moisture were created by simply varying the original basin depth, then backfilling uniformly with my marsh soil.

The last and most enjoyable task was plant selection. Since butterflies and hummingbirds both ranked high in my plans, I factored in their needs with questions of plant size, fragrance, hardiness, color, and seasonal interest.

Spicebush, sweet pepperbush, buttonbush, silky dogwood, and wafer ash will someday tower over cardinal flower, arrowhead, swamp milkweed, and pickerelweed. Joepyeweed looms over the downstream end of the marsh, providing a transition between the marsh and the butterfly garden.

Nature will take over from here. I plan on sitting down, resting my back, and watching wildlife move into my side yard marsh.

Many Uses of Marigolds

Many gardeners followed the battle over the choice of our national flower. In the end, the rose beat the marigold, but only, perhaps, by a nose. For wildlife-minded gardeners, the marigold is every bit as desirable as the rose and betters it in several ways.

Yard patrol is one of my gardening joys. Armed with binoculars for spying on the avian and lepidopteran denizens of my quarter acre, I spend hours meandering: checking out the shadbush crop, looking for the monarch eggs on milkweeds, verifying that first mourning warbler back in the scrubby tangle that marks the property line.

Marigolds aren't finicky plants and roses are. Too many roses means less meandering time. Therefore, I plant hundreds of marigolds. They thrive in full sun, average to poor soil, and bloom continuously if you keep seeds from forming. Marigolds provide nectar for butterflies and seeds for juncos and sparrows. Some marigold varieties offer a degree of nematode and insect control, but remember to choose carefully. Here is a brief evaluation of several species:

French marigold *(Tagetes patula)*. Despite its name, this flower is a Western Hemisphere native, as are all other marigolds. More than 200 varieties are available, but if you want but-terflies, choose single blooms, such as Naughty Marietta, or those just barely double. The size of the flower is not important. Hybrids such as Burpee's Mules or Park's Hi-Gs offer wildlife almost nothing but do sport large flowers that are incredibly long-lasting. Thompson and Morgan offers the best line of single French marigolds.

African marigold *(T. erecta)*. It is the tallest of the clan, but has little value to wildlife. Breeders took the wild single-flowered form and bred out most of its capability to produce nectar and seeds.

Signet marigold *(T. tenuifolia)*. Although relatively unknown to many gardeners, this is a plant to try. The flowers are single and small but numerous. They attract some butterflies and many other beneficial insects. Its seed is small and slender and is of limited bird feeding value. Thompson and Morgan carries four varieties.

Sweet-scented marigold *(T. lucida)*. Not great in bloom and not a plant whose seeds a cardinal can chow down on, but *you* can eat it! This herb is grown by native Americans in the southwestern United States. With a smell somewhere between anise and tarragon, it's worth a try.

Irish lace marigold *(T. filifolia)*. My source is a naturalized Nebraska population of this Central American flower, but you can find it in your Park's catalog. Grow it as a border for its lacy foliage, which is sweetly pungent. The flowers will go nearly unnoticed, but I'll bet it's a great insect repeller. Try it!

Before the last leaves fall from my trees and shrubs, I give myself a break from more mundane gardening chores and treat myself to a treasure hunt. I enjoy attracting wildlife to my landscape but can't always find room in our budget for the diversity of excellent trees and shrubs available at local garden centers. You'll find a treasure hunt to be good medicine for your spirit, your landscape, and local wildlife.

For years, birds and mammals have visited your yard, night and day. Left behind in their droppings is a wealth of seeds. Last winter primed many of those seeds for spring growth. With spring's warmth and rains, seedlings grew and now dot your planting beds. You can dismiss them as weeds, or you can treasure and transplant the ones which show promise.

I pot two to three dozen shrub and tree seedlings annually as a result of my treasure hunts. Eventually two or three will find their way into my landscape. I'll use others to revegetate an adjacent common ground. The remainder will come in handy as house gifts or as barter with other wildlife gardeners.

Autumn is the ideal time for transplanting or planting most trees and shrubs. As its leaves drop, the plant seems to go dormant. Below the soil, however, its root system is rapidly growing, anchoring the stems against winter winds and priming the plant for spring's burst of flower and leaf.

Keep a healthy supply of plastic pots on hand. Fill a two-quart pot with a good soil mix. Plant the seedling, water it well, and set it in a weather-exposed yet sheltered spot. Next fall, these plants will have doubled or tripled in size. You can either repot them or move them into your landscape.

With limited time and space to care for these waifs, I've learned to be selective in my choice of keepers. Native species top my list. They are difficult to find in nurseries. Unless I am part of an officially recognized salvage operation, I never dig them from the wild.

Seedlings from your yard grow under good garden conditions. By transplanting them early in their lives, they will make much better landscape plants than even properly salvaged larger specimens or root-bound stock from a nursery.

The green gold that I find will differ from your treasure. Judicious bartering can bring you the diversity you want. This year, hackberry, an excellent food tree for a number of butterfly caterpillars and birds, was my best find. Some Eastern redcedars and wild black cherries were yanked as weeds, but I transplanted the best of each.

Foxes have introduced persimmon to my yard. I'll trade these seedlings for pawpaw, whose leaves mean life to the beautiful zebra swallowtail butterfly and whose fruits will provide tasty, late summer treats to the countless small mammals that visit my yard.

Sprouting from Scratch

Sometimes it can be quite a challenge to get seeds to sprout. As an addicted collector of seeds from native plants, (particularly seeds of plants that attract wildlife), I've had to resort to some ingenious, not to say abusive methods to trick seeds into germinating. Since I tend to think of every seed as an egg, more or less, I sometimes feel somewhat uncomfortable that one doesn't treat seeds as gently and carefully as one treats eggs.

Generally speaking, many seeds must go through two important processes before they'll sprout: stratification and scarification. Seeds from a seed house are all primed and ready to go—given a healthy supply of light, warmth, and moisture (except those seeds that sprout best in the dark).

To germinate, the seeds of many trees, shrubs, and flowers have to go through a cool, moist period, a process called stratification. In nature, simply lying on the ground, with repeated freezing and thawing, softens some seed coats mechanically so that they sprout when the weather turns warm.

To duplicate this process with seeds collected in the fall for spring planting, I've sometimes left them outside in a pot through the winter. I've also put them in moist sphagnum moss and refrigerated them for 60 to 90 days. In this way, I've stratified milkweed seeds (the mainstay of my butterfly-gardening efforts), thereby increasing their rate of germination.

Scarification, the thinning of seed coats by scarring, must be done before stratification. It occurs for many seeds as they pass through the digestive tracts of birds or mammals. This process is a little harder to duplicate indoors, but it can be done either by rubbing the seeds back and forth on sandpaper or by nicking them with pliers. Pouring boiling water over the seeds the day before they're planted and letting them steep overnight also scarifies them. The process releases that germination trigger—especially with seeds from plants in the bean family such as wild senna, Kentucky coffee tree, wisteria, and goats' rue. Seeds that under normal circumstances must pass through the strong acids of digestive systems may need a dose of concentrated sulphuric acid to induce them to sprout.

You see what I mean about seed abuse! You may balk at these treatments yet want to provide plants whose fruit is loved by birds in your neighborhood. If so, there's one way to collect native seed that's as ready to germinate as packaged seed: clean out your gutters in March. Bird droppings will have gathered there through the cold months. Seeds already scarified by the birds will have been stratified through a series of gutter freezes and thaws. Sort the now clean seeds and see what sprouts. It's a sure-fire way to come up with plants that attract your local birds.

A rose is a rose is a rose . . . sometimes. For the wildlife gardener, the word rose brings to mind either wonderfully scented, beautifully flowering mounds of lush green foliage sustained only through minute by minute fungicide applications, or that much maligned but wonderful habitat resource, the rampant multiflora. Isn't there a middle ground—a floriferous, easy to care for, densely shrubby rose? Yes, there are the rugosas and native species such as the prairie, swamp, and pasture roses. But they are not for everyone. Rugosas are sometimes fussy and the natives are hard to come by.

However, a 1987 All-America Rose selection offers lots of bloom over a period of months. It is very hardy, practically care free, densely shrubby, and bears heavy crops of hips through the fall and into the winter. This seeming miracle is the Bonica shrub rose.

What does this rose look like? Think of a multiflora which stays fairly compact, 4 feet high by 5 feet wide. Add hundreds of pink flowers per plant, each 2 to 3 inches in diameter, fully double and slightly fragrant. Frame the flowers against deep green, glossy foliage. That's a rough sketch of the Bonica shrub rose.

The Bonica may not be a breakthrough plant for rose breeders but it gives residential and commercial landscapes a boost. It's the result of crossing the unnamed seedling of a climber, the evergreen rose, and a rambler named Mlle. Marthe Carron, pollinated by the well-known floribunda, Picasso. The original cross was made by the French rose breeder, the House of Meilland. This new rose was tested for years in the United States. It flourished through severe winters, summer heat, drought, and pestilence that would have killed lesser plants. This rose was introduced into the U.S. horticultural trade by the Conard-Pyle Company.

In summer, the rose provides ideal nesting habitat for mockingbirds, song sparrows, cardinals, and catbirds. In winter, a grouping of three or more Bonicas placed near your bird feeders offers safe harbor for many species of songbirds waiting their turn for a sunflower, millet, or niger seed snack.

The abundant flowers will attract nectar and pollen diners, which, in turn, will entice insect-eating birds. The abundant half-inch long fruits or hips, the product of summer insect pollination, turn orange-red in September. They hold their color well, providing winter landscape interest.

These fruits provide food for birds and mammals through January.

My wildlife-attracting yard is beginning to burst at the seams. Bonica seems so good, however, that I know I'll find a spot for it. The birds will thank me in their own way. As you visit your garden center, look for this new rose—then find a home for it in your landscape. You'll be glad you did.

A Bloomin' Ground Cover

Violets are beautiful, flowering ground covers, especially wherever they can be contained within planting beds. In moist, shady areas, violets might replace the traditional grasses commonly used as ground covers.

I've been introducing violets into my yard for a year now. You can choose from many varieties: more than 70 species native to the United States, plus another 50 or 60 kinds if you count European varieties and horticultural cultivars.

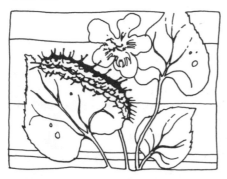

Violets come in many shades, from the multicolor pansies to the sweet, fragrant whites and tall-stemmed yellows, blues, purples, lavenders, and magentas. A good way to start collecting violets is to get your friends to share their plantings; they will always have plenty to spare.

We expect to see violets growing in somewhat shady places. Some violets, however, grow in well-drained, barren, hot spots or in prairies. The birdsfoot violet, *Viola pedata*, one of the most desirable native species, has a thick, stubby, vertical root resembling that of the beautiful butterfly weed. Because of this upright root system, birdsfoot violets do not exhibit the rampant spreading of other kinds.

Besides providing effective ground cover, violets are most useful to butterflies—particularly those large orange, black, and silver species known as fritillaries. This large group ranges across the United States and southern Canada and may first be drawn to your yard by buddleia, milkweeds, thistles, and other plants that you may grow for the nectar they provide the adults. It's when these beautiful butterflies lay their eggs, however, that violets become a vital link in the butterflies' annual life cycle.

In the fall, many female fritillaries lay their eggs on or near the violets. The violets' leaves and flowers are the primary food of the caterpillars when they begin to feed in the spring. The young caterpillars are often orange-and black-striped. As they mature, they may become nocturnal munchers, so you'll see them only if you poke around your violets at night.

Other kinds of butterflies, such as the falcate orange-tip, and other insects may seek out violets for their early spring nectar.

Other creatures, too, find violets tasty. Violet-eating rabbits may actually be allies, since their persistent eating can retard the too-rapid spreading of the violets—without seriously harming the lush violet carpeting. Cardinals and other birds avidly seek out the violets' numerous seeds.

To tell the truth, I like to snack on violets too—the leaves and especially the flowers. Some people like violets candied as a condiment. I prefer them as a garden snack—plain, plucked from my insecticide-free garden and popped in my mouth and munched—just like a rabbit would do!

How about Amelanchiers?

Amelanchiers (am' el an' kē ers), members of the rose family, are native trees and shrubs that should find a place in most home landscapes. They bloom early and provide fruit long before most other plants. They also attract a variety of native songbirds and other wildlife to your yard.

The fruit is as tasty to people as it is to birds. One of my fondest memories is of a July afternoon spent sitting on the banks of the Little Beaver Kill in New York State's Catskill Mountains. Having exhausted most of the possibilities of catching brown trout, I was relaxing underneath a tree-sized amelanchier, sharing lots of the incredibly sweet purple-red fruit with cedar waxwings and Baltimore orioles.

Throughout much of the United States, 10 to 15 species of amelanchier (also known as serviceberry, sarvis, shadbush, and shadblow) are fairly commonplace in the natural environment. We may rarely notice them, except in the early spring when their billows of starry white flowers brighten the still rather austere landscape.

Over the past 10 years or so, some of the plants, notably *Amelanchier canadensis* and *Amelanchier laevis*, have found their way to many local nurseries. These plants feature tasty fruit, excellent spring flowers, attractive bark and, sometimes, red or yellow fall foliage. Few disease problems plague these hardy plants.

Put some amelanchiers (often called "shads") in your yard. Their flowers may attract some of the butterflies that emerge earliest, such as the larger swallowtails, the blues, the whites, some hairstreaks, and elfins.

Songbirds will make the most use of your shads, feasting on the ripe fruits.

Visitors may include orioles, tanagers, certainly cardinals and robins, plus mockingbirds, yellow-breasted chats, catbirds, thrushes, and thrashers, as well as occasional game birds such as quail and turkey.

The type and size of a shadbush should be keyed to the size of your property and its soil conditions. Some amelanchiers are small shrubs (4 or 5 feet in height) and grow upright in clumps. At the other extreme are species such as *Amelanchier canadensis*

and *Amelanchier arborea* which grow into 10- to 30-foot trees. In time, the trees will probably develop three or four trunks, growing together closely the way clump birch and witch hazel trees grow. A few amelanchiers prefer wet soils; others grow on the driest of rocky slopes.

Some amelanchiers are available through mail order catalogs; others can be obtained only through specialty nurseries. The wonderful shadbush is well worth a perusal of your winter catalog or a visit to your garden center.

Whether you're concerned with the plants' form and color or, like millions of other Americans, you'd like to entice songbirds to your yard, amelanchiers make an excellent landscape choice.

Gourmet Herbs for Wildlife

Herbs—those fragrant plants that add texture to our gardens and zing to our cooking—are also of great value to wildlife.

I used to be able to count on one hand the herbs that I grew—a clump of chives, enough parsley for a season or two of garnishes, and sweet basil for the two dozen quarts of tomato sauce we put up each year. Then I found many others that smelled and looked good. Lavender made its way into our closets. Lemon balm found a place in iced tea.

Many flowers and vegetables benefit from being close to "companion" herb plants such as sage, thyme, oregano, garlic, chives, and wormwood. The strong scent of these herbs protects neighboring plants from insect pests. An insect (usually attracted by both the sight and smell of a plant) may fix its eyes on a squash, only to find on arrival that what looks like squash smells like the nearby offensive sage and not at all like tasty squash. Confusing! Some other herbs literally drive insects off, and some contain chemicals that inhibit insects' growth or actually kill certain pests. Such natural pest control is far better for other backyard wildlife than the use of pesticides.

Considerable care is needed in choosing the right herbs as companions for flowers and vegetables, since some plants are harmed rather than helped by certain herbs.

Some varieties of butterflies, especially small, fast-flying skippers, are drawn to herbs such as sage, thyme, hyssop, catnip, borage, and lavender. These herbs provide nectar. Caterpillars of other butterflies (swallowtails such as the Eastern and short-tailed black varieties, and the desert and anise kind) make their homes on (and eat the leaves of) certain herbs in the parsley family, such as carrot, fennel, angelica, dill, and chervil.

To produce the most butterflies with minimal caterpillar damage to individual herbs, gently spread the voracious caterpillars around. That way they can feed evenly throughout your herb plants.

Many hummingbirds are attracted to certain herbs, including Mexican bush sage, pineapple sage, and beebalm *(Monarda didyma)*. Beebalm, a hardy herb also known as Oswego tea, can be grown throughout much of the United States. The sages mentioned, although not winter-hardy, can be cut back and brought inside for the winter; move them outside again in the spring.

Even the seeds of some herbs appeal to certain birds. If you allow some herbs, particularly catnip and sage, to go to seed, you're likely to attract birds such as goldfinches. There's nothing niftier than spotting a goldfinch probing through withered flowerheads of catnip in search of tasty seeds.

Early fall is probably the best time to evaluate your landscaping. What has been growing successfully throughout the spring and summer? What's been struggling along for two or three years, in spite of your best efforts? Should some of the trees that dominate your yard be taken down to give more light and make room for more vegetables, shrubs, and/or perennials? And (most important) what plantings bring birds and butterflies to your yard? What plants do your local wildlife ignore?

My own yard is almost a year old now. I've been watching it turn from a barren piece of land to a young—though still awkward—landscape. I've been taking notes on what's going on in my 9,000 square feet of yard. I can see now that planting more evergreens for wildlife winter cover is a must. I'll probably put in some of the many holly varieties.

On the other hand, the purple leaf plum tree that came with the house probably has to go. Although it looks good, its fruit attracts insect pests instead of birds. I am thinking of replacing the plum with perhaps a Korean mountain ash *(Sorbus alnifolia)* which produces many berries well into winter and creates few pest problems.

Along with my usual fall chores (including the replanting of the tulip bulbs I dug up in June, giving the bulb beds a healthy dose of bone meal), I'll soon be planting some shrubs I've been nursing along.

Last winter I collected a variety of cuttings from shrubs that provide good food or cover for wildlife. I then kept the cuttings refrigerated in damp peat moss until April when I put them out in a planting bed. In June, I transplanted them to individual containers. Soon they will go into the ground. I'll group them by threes and fives; each group will eventually occupy about 60 to 100 square feet, replacing much of what is now lawn. These shrubs include:

Buttonbush *(Cephalanthus occidentalis)*. This dense wetland shrub also grows well in yards and provides food and nesting cover for birds. Its fragrant flowers attract butterflies and hummingbirds.

American elderberry *(Sambucus canadensis)*. It has clusters of large white flowers in May and June and

black berries in July and August. The berries appeal to birds as well as to those of us who like good homemade pies and elderberry wine. The fall foliage is attractive.

Silky dogwood *(Cornus amomum)*. This shrub has dense reddish or purple twigs that are good for nesting. Its May/June creamy-white flowers often attract the spring azure butterflies, and its blue berries attract birds from September through November. Its lovely foliage is scarlet.

How's *your* yard doing as habitat for both you and your wildlife? Early fall is a good time to take stock.

Becoming a Wildlife Lister

If you've never before listed your wildlife observations, winter is an ideal time to begin: your yard is fairly quiet and your note-taking can get off to a comfortable, leisurely start.

Watching the comings and goings of wildlife visitors turns into an enjoyable and profitable game when you actually list the changes brought about by the seasons. Make a chart and fasten it to a clipboard kept alongside your favorite wildlife-watching window or next to the door between your house and yard.

You can put your notes in columns: numbers and names of species; description; date observed; time of day; place (which part of yard); and activity (feeding, digging, nesting, pecking at a dead tree, etc.). If you have a computer, you might like to set up a data base for all your information. That's how I keep track of unfolding patterns.

Even though birds will be the most common visitors, you'll want to note what goes on in the world of insects, mammals, reptiles, and amphibians. Your observations can even take in surrounding fields, woods, or streets,

if you like. Friends of mine have kept track of large birds of prey and migrating waterfowl that would probably not ever enter their yard, yet are certainly part of their personal world.

Within the past year, as my garden has developed, I've noted 23 species of butterflies and skippers, in both caterpillar and adult stages. I've even specified what shape each individual is in. My notes tell me, for example, that when most of the tiger swallowtail butterflies take on a faded, tattered look in late June, they are near the end of their life. I discovered, too, that it's late summer before the caterpillars of the variegated fritillaries show up in my area.

And just this past October, while checking over my plantings, I noticed small, pale, blackheaded, yellow-green caterpillars nesting in the leaves of my native columbines, the tops of which were chewed off. My books told me this was the caterpillar of the locally rare columbine skipper, which feeds only on columbines. It winters in nests among dead columbine leaves and emerges in spring as an attractive black, beige, and white butterfly which will lay eggs on the spring columbine shoots. I was glad not to have swept the leaves into the compost heap!

Keeping notes and checking authoritative books for answers lays the groundwork for identifying patterns of growth and behavior. It may be a game, but it can also help make your yard a better place to welcome wildlife.

About the Author

Craig Tufts didn't invent the idea of planting certain flowers, shrubs, and trees to attract animals, but he is one of the leading experts and most ardent practitioners of gardening for wildlife. This book compiles selections from his nationally distributed column, *The Backyard Naturalist*. Tufts has also appeared numerous times on television including over a dozen appearances interviewing wildlife gardeners throughout the United States on Public Television's *The Victory Garden*. He has written articles on this topic for *Wild Bird* magazine and in *Taylor's Guide to Natural Landscaping* and has assisted in editing numerous other publications on the topic.

At the National Wildlife Federation, he manages the Backyard Wildlife Habitat Program, which began in 1973 as an effort to encourage people to create and to enhance places for wildlife to live. Now more than 12,000 Americans have had their properties certified by NWF as official Backyard Wildlife Habitats. To be certified, wildlife enthusiasts landscape their yards to provide four major wildlife needs: food, water, cover, and places to raise young.

Program participants have described their efforts to newspaper and magazine writers throughout the country. They include city dwellers who set up mini-refuges in tiny urban plots as well as suburbanites and rural citizens who create extensive wildlife landscapes that contain such wildlife amenities as expansive pond and artificial stream complexes, bat and butterfly roosting boxes, and even bird saunas for wintertime bird bathing.

Many Program participants become active in their communities soon after their certification. Backyard Wildlifers work on habitat projects at schools, businesses and in retirement communities. They may assist as educators at nature centers, as land managers at natural heritage sites or as organizers of community action projects ranging from reform of town ordinances to green space preservation efforts.

Tufts holds degrees in wildlife conservation and environmental education from Cornell University. With his family, he shares a 9,000 square foot lot in northern Virginia that features over 200 native plant species, a big vegetable garden, wildlife pond, and a great many wildlife visitors—butterflies, birds, frogs, box turtles, mammals and countless others—that have discovered top-quality habitat in a fairly typical suburban neighborhood.

To let your friends, family and neighbors know about how they can develop their own National Wildlife Federation Backyard Wildlife Habitat, ask them to order our Backyard Wildlife Habitat information packet by calling 1-800-432-6564.

Index